HAWAII

HAWAII BY ROAD

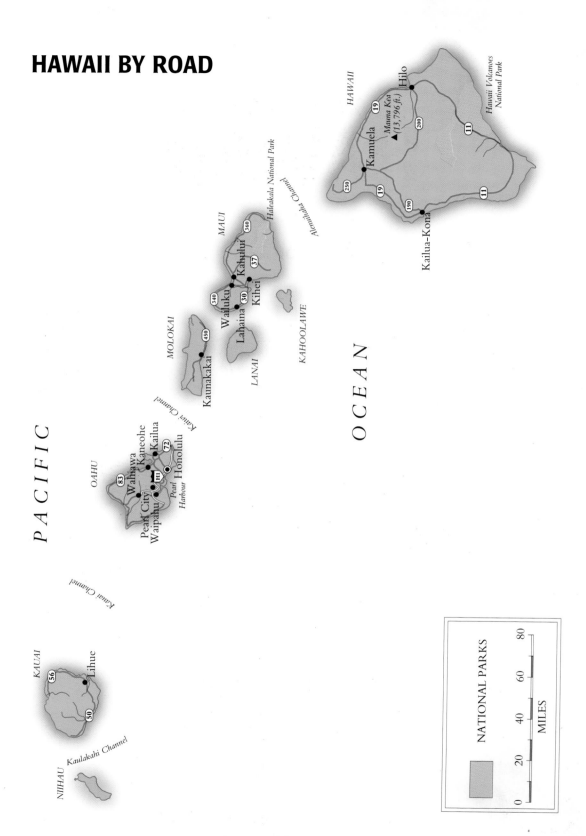

HAWAII

Hilo

Mauna Kea
(13,796 ft.)

Kamuela

19

200

111

Hawaii Volcanoes
National Park

250

19

190

111

Kailua-Kona

Haleakala National Park

MAUI

360

Kahului

37

340

Wailuku

30

Lahaina

Kihei

Alenuihaha Channel

KAHOOLAWE

OCEAN

MOLOKAI

450

Kaunakakai

LANAI

Kauai Channel

PACIFIC

OAHU

Wahiawa

Kaneohe

Kailua

72

83

Pearl City

Waipahu

Honolulu

*Pearl
Harbour*

Kauai Channel

KAUAI

56

Lihue

50

Kaulakahi Channel

NIIHAU

NATIONAL PARKS

MILES

0   20   40   60   80

CELEBRATE THE STATES
HAWAII

Jake Goldberg

BENCHMARK BOOKS

MARSHALL CAVENDISH
NEW YORK

Benchmark Books
Marshall Cavendish Corporation
99 White Plains Road
Tarrytown, New York 10591-9001

Library of Congress Cataloging-in-Publication Data
Goldberg, Jake.
Hawaii / Jake Goldberg.
p.   cm.   (Celebrate the states)
Includes bibliographical references (p.   ) and index.
Summary: Describes the geography, history, government, economy, people,
and culture of this island state.
ISBN 0-7614-0203-9 (lib. bdg.)
1. Hawaii—Juvenile literature. [1. Hawaii.] I. Title. II. Series.
DU623.G563   1998   996.9—dc21   96-51536   CIP   AC

Maps and graphics supplied by Oxford Cartographers, Oxford, England

Photo Research by Ellen Barrett Dudley and Matthew J. Dudley

Cover photo: *Tom Stack & Associates*, Dave B. Fleetham

The photographs in this book are used by permission and through the courtesy of: *Photo Researchers, Inc.*:
Jan Halaska, 6-7, 127; Jeff Greenberg, 17, 70-71, 114; Porterfield-Chickering, 19, 74; Wayne Scherr, 26;
J.H. Robinson, 27; Francois Gohier, 29, 88; Frans Lanting, 30; David R. Frazier, 68 (bottom), 116-117;
Andy Levin, 73; K.W. Fink, 75; Sylvain Cazenave, 82; Tim Davis, 111; Stephen J. Kraseman, 121 (top). *The
Image Bank*: David Hamilton, 10-11; Eric Meola, 15; Benn Mitchell, 20; Alvis Upitis, 24 (top and bottom);
Cindy Turner, 61; Turner & De Vries, 65; Jay Freis, 68 (top); Alan Becker, 78; John Lewis Stage, 80, 90-91;
Kaz Mori, 81, 105; Don King, 118; H. Sund, 129; Grant V. Faint, back cover. *Tom Stack & Associates*: Mark
Newman, 14; Brian Parker, 21; Greg Vaughn, 23, 54-55, 85, 109, 110, 138; Ed Robinson, 102-103; Michael
Nolan, 115; Dave B. Fleetham, 124. *Bishop Museum*: 32-33, 35, 37, 38, 39, 41, 44, 45, 49, 53, 130, 131, 133
(left and right), 136; Charles Furneaux, 47; United Japanese Society, 52; Ray Jerome, 100; J.J. Williams, 132;
Seth Joel, 134. *George Kodama*: 57. *Verner, Liipfert, Bernhard McPherson and Hand*: 58. *Hawaii Visitors
and Convention Bureau*: Amos Nachoum, 77; Asia/Pacific, 86; Lyon Arboretum, 121 (bottom). *UPI/Corbis-
Bettmann*: 93, 94. *Reuters/Corbis-Bettmann*: 96. *Corbis-Bettmann*: 97. *Paul C. Drews/© Kathleen Tyau*: 99.

Printed in Italy

1   3   5   6   4   2

CONTENTS

HAWAII IS . . . .

Hawaii is a place of rare beauty.

"The loveliest fleet of islands that lies anchored to any ocean."
—Writer Mark Twain

"If anyone desires such old-fashioned things as lovely scenery, quiet, pure air, clear sea water, good food and heavenly sunsets . . . I recommend him cordially to [Waikiki Beach]."
—Writer Robert Louis Stevenson

Hawaii has a troubled past . . .

"It is our imperative duty to hold these islands with the invincible strength of the American nation."
—U.S. minister to Hawaii John L. Stevens, 1892

"The people of the islands have no voice in determining their future, but are virtually relegated to the condition of the aborigines of the American Continent. An alien element composed of men of energy and determination control all the resources of Honolulu and will employ them tirelessly to secure their ends."
—Queen Liliuokalani

. . . with a bright and unique future among the fifty states.

"Being Hawaiian today is finally feeling at home after nearly a century of trying to live like foreigners told us we should live in our own land."
—Community leader Abby Napeahi

"The Congress apologizes to Native Hawaiians on behalf of the people of the United States for the overthrow of the Kingdom of Hawaii on January 17, 1893 . . . and the deprivation of the rights of Native Hawaiians to self-determination."
—United States Public Law 103–150, as signed
by President Bill Clinton on November 23, 1993

"Hawaii is unique in its combination of beauty in the natural physical environment, in its people and their Aloha spirit, and in its cosmopolitan mixing of ethnic groups, cultures, religions, and lifestyles. These facets of beauty are to be preserved and enhanced, not only because they are the basis of attraction to visitors but because they are the basis for Hawaii's attraction to its own people."
—State of Hawaii Tourism Policy Act

America's Pacific island gem, Hawaii, stands alone among the fifty states in many ways. It did not become a state until 1959, and its ocean setting, gentle climate, spectacular beauty, distance from the continental United States, and mixture of peoples and backgrounds sometimes make it seem more like an exotic foreign land than one of the states. Yet in the challenges it faces—and the optimism with which it welcomes the future—Hawaii is unmistakably American.

1 THE ISLAND STATE

The state of Hawaii lies in the middle of the Pacific Ocean, almost midway between Asia and America. It sits more than two thousand miles away from the mainland of the United States, the nation of which it is a part. Hawaii is an archipelago, or a chain of islands, that stretches in a crescent shape over more than fifteen hundred miles of ocean, from the island of Hawaii itself, in the southeast, to the tiny island of Kure, in the northwest.

SUNSHINE AND RAIN

Hawaii's climate is warm and tropical. There is little difference in the weather between summer and winter. Throughout the year, temperatures in the lowlands are in the seventies and eighties during the day and drop to the sixties at night. "Our kids love going to school in Hawaii because they get to go barefoot, and they only have to wear shorts and T-shirts, even in the winter," says Tim Starr, who recently moved to the island of Maui from Minnesota.

Most of the time, steady northeasterly trade winds blow moisture from the Pacific across the islands. The air dries when it encounters Hawaii's volcanic peaks and mountain ranges. The result is warm, wet weather on the northeastern, or windward, side of the volcanic peaks and hot, dry weather on the western, or leeward, side. That

LAND AND WATER

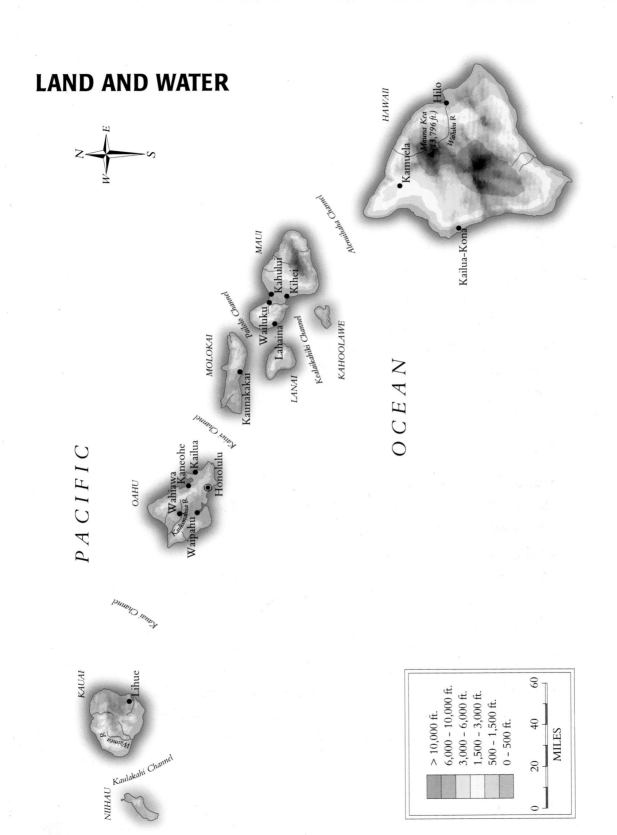

accounts for the island's incredible geographical contrasts between dense, wet rain forests and dry, sandy beaches.

BORN OF FIRE

The Hawaiian Islands were formed tens of millions of years ago by volcanic eruptions. At that time, the thin crust of the earth under the ocean began to break apart. Hot, molten lava flowed from deep within the earth through the cracks.

As lava solidifies, the top layer often cools first. This results in pockets that are like pudding: they have a stiff skin on top and runnier, softer lava underneath.

LAND OF VOLCANOES

Hawaii's volcanoes very rarely erupt explosively, the way Mount Saint Helens did in Washington State. Instead, when heat and pressure build up deep inside the earth, hot lava pours freely down the sides of the volcanic cone, building up its height and size. Sometimes the lava oozes all the way down the mountainsides and reaches the ocean, where it is cooled and forms new land. Since Kilauea volcano on the island of Hawaii began spewing lava regularly in 1983, the island has grown five hundred acres larger.

Kilauea's lava usually flows slowly down its slopes, so people have time to get out of the way. Only one person has been killed since 1983, but the molten rock, which reaches eighteen hundred degrees, has burned down nearly two hundred homes. After so many years of living in the volcano's shadow, Hawaiians are used to it. "I don't worry about the volcano," says Phil Henderson, who works in Hilo, thirty miles from Kilauea, "although it's exciting, new earth being formed."

Solidified by the cool ocean waters, the lava flows formed immense underwater mountains. Over time, as the lava continued to bubble up, these grew and grew, until they had risen above the ocean and formed dry land. This land is the Hawaiian Islands, the largest of all the Pacific island chains.

The volcanoes on the northern islands are mostly dormant (inactive for now) or extinct. But two volcanoes on the island of Hawaii—Mauna Loa and Kilauea—are active, still pouring out flows of lava to create new land.

In fact, to the south of the island of Hawaii a new island is now forming. Though it is still several thousand feet below the surface of the ocean and not expected to emerge from the sea for another ten thousand years, Hawaiians have already given it a name: Loihi.

EIGHT ISLANDS

There are 132 islands, reefs, and shoals in the Hawaiian archipelago, but only 8 are considered of major importance. Those are the islands of Hawaii, Maui, Kahoolawe, Lanai, Molokai, Oahu, Kauai, and Niihau.

Hawaii. With an area of more than four thousand square miles, the island of Hawaii is known as the Big Island. The peaks of its two largest volcanoes—Mauna Kea, at 13,796 feet, and Mauna Loa, at 13,677 feet—are high enough to be covered by snow in winter. The sky above Mauna Kea is so clear and the air so pure that astronomers regard the summit of the volcano as one of the best places on earth to observe the heavens.

To the east of Mauna Kea is beautiful Akaka Falls, the highest

At 420 feet, Akaka Falls is Hawaii's tallest waterfall.

waterfall in the state. Along the southeast side of the island is the steaming crater of Kilauea, now part of Hawaii Volcanoes National Park. The island's major city and port is Hilo, on the east coast.

Hawaii is noted for its black sand beaches, which are made of pulverized lava. Near Ka Lae, the southern tip of the island and the southernmost point anywhere in United States territory, there is also a beach of green sand. This peculiar sand was created when a lava flow released a large vein of the mineral olivine.

Maui. To the northeast of Hawaii lies Maui, the second-largest island in the Hawaiian archipelago. Maui is shaped somewhat like an hourglass. The northwestern lobe of the island is dominated by the volcano called Puu Kukui; the southeastern lobe, by Haleakala, the largest dormant volcano in the world.

The central valley that connects the two lobes and gives Maui its nickname, the Valley Island, is the island's residential and business center. Sugarcane, pineapples, and other crops are grown there.

Kahoolawe. The tiny island of Kahoolawe lies south of Maui. The smallest of the major Hawaiian Islands, it is uninhabited. In the 1800s, it was used as a penal colony and as pastureland for grazing sheep. During much of the twentieth century, the U.S. Navy used it for target practice. In 1994, the navy returned control of the island to the state of Hawaii. Currently, the navy is trying to clean up Kahoolawe by removing unexploded shells.

Lanai. Fewer than three thousand people live on the small island of Lanai. Its highest point is Lanaihale, a 3,370-foot-high mountain on the eastern coast. The main town, Lanai City, is located in the center of the island. Lanai is sometimes called the

Vast sugarcane plantations cover Maui's central valley.

Pineapple Island. It was there, in 1922, that James Dole of the famous pineapple family established his fifteen-thousand-acre pineapple plantation. Today, the economy of Lanai is in the midst of a rapid transition from pineapple production to tourism.

Molokai. Northwest of Maui lies the island of Molokai, home to the world's tallest sea cliffs. For a long time Molokai was known as the Lonely Island. People were afraid to stop there because of the leper colony that was established on the Kalaupapa Peninsula in

Dole pineapple owns 98 percent of Lanai, which is known as Pineapple Island.

1866. Leprosy causes scales and sores on the skin and deforms body parts. Because the disease is infectious, lepers were forced to live apart from everyone else. Modern medicine has done much to control leprosy, and the government began phasing out the leper colony on Molokai in 1957. Today, Molokai is often called the Friendly Isle.

Oahu. To the west of Molokai lies Oahu. Though it only covers about six hundred square miles, Oahu is the most heavily populated island. More than 830,000 people live there, which amounts to about 75 percent of the state's population. Oahu is dominated by two mountain ranges, the Waianae range along the western coast and the Koolau mountains to the east.

In the southeastern corner of the island is the city of Honolulu, the state capital. Honolulu is also Hawaii's principal port, the site of its major international airport, and the business and financial center of the state. On the southern side of the city is Waikiki Beach, a mecca for tourists from around the world. To the west is

Waikiki has long been a tourist destination. Today, high-rise hotels tower over the narrow beach.

Pearl Harbor. That is the site of the American naval base that the Japanese bombed in 1941, provoking the United States to enter World War II.

Kauai. Known as the Garden Island, Kauai is often thought to be the most beautiful of the Hawaiian Islands. The entire island of Kauai was formed from the single eruption of a large volcano. It has a rugged, mountainous interior with steep valleys and gorges. These are surrounded by white, sandy beaches along the coast. Wrapped in clouds much of the time, the mountains are wet and covered in lush vegetation. The most spectacular valley on Kauai is Waimea Canyon on the western side of the island. Ten miles long, a mile wide, and a half mile deep, Waimea has been called a mini Grand Canyon.

Niihau. The tiny island of Niihau lies seventeen miles west of Kauai. Its seventy-two square miles are privately owned. Today it is home to fewer than three hundred people, mostly cattle ranchers and farmers. Niihau is important, though, because it has the largest concentration of pure-blooded Polynesian Hawaiians left in the entire state. Hawaiian is still taught in the schools of Niihau as the primary language.

A COLORFUL WORLD

Throughout Hawaii, flowers and trees bloom in a rainbow of colors, making the islands seem a lush paradise. Yellow hibiscus, the state flower, is a tropical shrub that flourishes all over the islands. Another common plant is bougainvillea, with blooms of purple, magenta, pink, and white. Then there are yellow ginger, red anthur-

Waimea Canyon, a colorful 2,000-foot gorge, has sometimes been called the Grand Canyon of the Pacific.

mium, orange trumpet vine, and many colors of orchids. Pikake is a variety of jasmine that is often used in leis, the wreaths of flowers that are draped around the necks of newcomers to the islands. The fragrant frangipani is also frequently used in leis. Profusions of brightly colored flowers adorn streets and homes and public places and fill the air with their pungent scent.

Hawaii is home to many
varieties of dazzling orchids.

Many of Hawaii's trees
blossom in lush colors, such
as the lavender of the
jacaranda tree.

Many of the tropical trees that grow in Hawaii's forests also produce beautiful flowers. The jacaranda tree has brilliant violet blossoms. The African tulip tree produces bright red flowers. The ohia, which also blooms in red, was thought to be a favorite of Pele, the fire goddess, and was considered sacred by the original Hawaiians. Equally brilliant are the flowers of the bauhinia and the wili-wili, or Australian umbrella tree. The royal poinciana was brought from Madagascar and produces bright scarlet blossoms, while the shower tree blooms in pink, coral, gold, and multicolored shades.

Some tropical trees also have practical uses. The wood of the hau and the milo is used for making canoes and bowls. The leaves of the pandanus and ti trees are used to weave mats and clothing. Tropical fruit trees furnish bananas, coconuts, litchi, macadamia nuts, papayas, guavas, pineapples, and mangoes. At Kona, on the island of Hawaii, you can find America's only commercial coffee plantation.

PROTECTING THE UNIQUE

For millions of years, the Hawaiian Islands were barren of all life. Strong Pacific winds, heavy tropical rains, and powerful ocean currents eroded the huge masses of lava, carving deep, razor-sharp valleys and high coastal cliffs out of the gently sloping mountains. In some parts of Hawaii, this volcanic landscape remains stark and sterile, so much so that in the 1960s the Apollo astronauts came to the dormant volcano of Haleakala on Maui to train for walking on the Moon.

Haleakala crater is a desolate, unearthly landscape.

But as time passed, most of the Hawaiian Islands were transformed into a lush paradise of exotic plants and animals. Seeds were carried there by the wind and by seabirds, and insects probably arrived on pieces of floating driftwood. In the warm and wet climate, these plant and animals flourished and multiplied, until the raw, lifeless, gray-and-black volcanic landscape was covered with thick vegetation in a thousand shades of green. Because of its geographical isolation, more than 90 percent of the plants and animals native to Hawaii are found nowhere else in the world.

For many centuries, no human eye looked upon Hawaii. But with the arrival of the Polynesians, followed by Europeans, Asians, and Americans, the islands' unusual ecosystem was changed forever. Today, many native Hawaiian species are extinct or near extinction because they were not as strong as those introduced by humans. Pigs, goats, and cats, brought by settlers and allowed to roam wild, have killed off many native species. These animals rove through the forests, eating and trampling delicate plants. "The feral pig is our worst enemy here," says Larry Katahira, who works at Hawaii Volcanoes National Park. "He knocks down the tree fern and chews out its starchy core heart, leaving a watery hollow where mosquitoes breed and carry disease to native birds."

Hawaiian birds had no natural predators, so they often nested on the ground. That made them easy prey when invaders arrived. Years ago, sugar plantation owners brought in small, ferretlike animals

Rooting through the forests, the feral pig has wreaked havoc on Hawaii's fragile native species.

called mongooses to control their rat problem. The mongooses ate bird eggs instead of rats. Today, only the island of Kauai, where the mongooses never became established, still has large populations of many species of native birds. In Kauai's rain forests you can still see such rare creatures as the 'a'o bird, which is no longer found on the other islands.

Insects and snakes that arrive on planes and boats also do much damage to Hawaii's fragile environment. Some insects infest and kill plants. Others carry diseases that are fatal to birds. Still others eat the larvae of the native bees and flies that are necessary to pollinate native plants. Even plants that settlers have brought in—from ornamental trees to blackberry bushes—can quickly crowd out the native species.

This invasion of foreign plants and animals has been catastrophic. The koloa, or Hawaiian duck, and the nene, or Hawaiian goose, are both endangered. The monk seal is seen only in remote areas of the islands, far from people. Half of Hawaii's species of birds are now extinct. Hawaii is home to 40 percent of the birds and 35 percent of the plants on the endangered species list for the entire United States. There are more than a hundred species of Hawaiian plants that have fewer than twenty individual specimens left.

Today, Hawaiians are keenly aware of the need to protect the remaining native species. Some are protected in special areas such as the Leeward Islands, a group of about a dozen tiny islands northwest of Niihau. Special permission is required to visit most of these islands, as they are part of the Hawaiian Islands National Wildlife Refuge and are home to millions of seabirds and endangered species such as the monk seal. Laysan Island, one of the Leewards,

THE MONK SEAL

The Hawaiian monk seal is found nowhere else in the world. More than fifteen million years old, it is the oldest of all the kinds of seals. There are two other species of monk seal, but only a few hundred Mediterranean monk seals remain and the Caribbean variety is already extinct. In the nineteenth century, explorers and seamen nearly killed off the Hawaiian species as well. Today, there are only about one thousand left, which live mostly on small, sandy islands in the northern part of the archipelago. Although nobody hunts these animals anymore, humans can still hurt them. The leading cause of death for monk seals is getting tangled up in fishnets, which prevents them from reaching the surface of the water to breathe. Boaters, fishers, and tourists will all have to cooperate to preserve this ancient creature.

Remote, unpopulated Laysan Island is home to the world's largest colony of albatrosses.

has the world's largest colony of albatrosses, though there used to be many more. In the last decade of the nineteenth century, it was discovered that the albumin in albatross eggs could be used to make a chemical useful in developing photographic film, and "egg-sweeping" parties greatly reduced the number of birds on the island.

Conservationists are trying to find ways to stem the tide of foreign species that enter on planes. Many of these creatures come from Guam. At the airport there, dogs sniff the cargo areas of planes, searching for snakes and other animals. But such efforts "are like bailing the ocean," says Mark White, of the Nature Conservancy of Hawaii. "We would like to see as much time, effort, and care put into screening cargo coming into Hawaii as in other states like California."

Other attempts have been more successful. On Maui, public and private landowners have cooperated to protect one hundred thousand acres of forest on the north slope of Haleakala Crater. "We have all joined forces to combine energy, money, and people intelligently," says Peter Baldwin, a local landowner. Under this program, fences have been erected around the most delicate sections of Haleakala to keep out the hungry feral pigs and goats. Hunting of these animals is also allowed. But park rangers still have to keep a vigilant eye on other nonactive species of plants and insects that are always creeping in.

In the future, such cooperation between public and private interests will be necessary to protect Hawaii's unique environment, so that both locals and tourists can continue to enjoy its rare and delicate beauty.

2 THE PAST IS PRESENT

Halemaumau by Charles Furneaux

The story of America's fiftieth state is rich in individual tales of uprooted peoples journeying to a strange new home; of striving to get along with people of many different backgrounds; of difficult, tedious, and dangerous years of labor at low wages; and of heroic efforts to create a better life. In all of this, the story of Hawaii is typically American.

THE FIRST HAWAIIANS

While the Hawaiian Islands were still unpopulated, events that would change it forever were taking place thousands of miles to the east, on the continent of Asia. Overpopulation and hostility from other tribes caused people from India, Myanmar, Thailand, and other areas to move to the tip of the Malaysian Peninsula. Eventually they crossed the waters to the thousands of Pacific islands called Indonesia.

There, they became expert fishermen and sailors and learned how to build large, ocean-going dugout canoes to travel from island to island. As they became ever more daring seamen, these people continued to migrate eastward into the region of the South Pacific known as Polynesia, which means "many islands."

About two thousand years ago, sailors from the Marquesas Islands in Polynesia set out across the ocean in search of new lands.

They traveled north across two thousand miles of open water, at a time when most European sailors were afraid to venture out of sight of land. Even today, the boldness of their journey astounds historians. "It was left to the men of the Pacific," wrote historical novelist James Michener, "to meet an ocean on its own terms and to conquer it. Lacking both metals and maps, sailing with only the stars . . . these men accomplished miracles."

After a long and perilous voyage, they came to a large, lush, inviting island. They believed that they had rediscovered the mythical paradise from which their people had originated, so they named the island Hawaii, as it was called in their ancient legend. By about A.D. 1200 they had settled throughout the Hawaiian archipelago.

Chiefs, or *alii*, who were believed to be descended from the

Ancient Hawaiian chiefs enjoyed many privileges. Here, a servant waves a fan to keep insects away from the chief.

gods, ruled over the common people with the help of the priests, or *kahunas*, who maintained order through an elaborate system of kapus, or taboos. The kapu system was oppressive. Commoners could not come too close to the chiefs, walk in their footsteps, touch their possessions, or cast a shadow on their property. Women could not prepare food for men or eat with them. The penalty for violation of the kapus was usually death. If a kapu was broken, however, a person was often allowed to escape to a designated sacred refuge, where a kahuna would absolve him of his sin. One of these ancient places is preserved at the City of Refuge National Historical Park on the Kona coast of the island of Hawaii.

The first Hawaiians lived off the riches of the sea and the cultivation of sweet potatoes, yams, and taro roots, which they had brought with them. They also brought dogs, pigs, and chickens from Southeast Asia, as well as bananas, sugarcane, coconuts, bamboo, and breadfruit.

CAPTAIN COOK

In January 1778, two ships, the *Resolution* and the *Discovery*, sailed into Waimea Bay on the island of Kauai. The vessels were under the command of Captain James Cook, an Englishman who had been sent to explore and map the South Pacific.

Cook called these islands that he had stumbled across the Sandwich Islands, after the Earl of Sandwich, who had sponsored his voyage. Cook only stayed for two weeks before sailing off, but after ten months he returned, hoping to repair his ships and get more food and supplies.

When Captain Cook first sailed into Waimea Bay, hundreds of Hawaiians rowed out to greet him.

At first, the Hawaiians marveled at the appearance of these *haoles*, or foreigners, fair-skinned men who wore a strange cloth skin all over their bodies. The British visitors were equally amazed at the welcome they received from the islanders. "I have nowhere in this sea seen such a number of people assembled in one place," Cook wrote in his journal. "Besides those in the canoes, all the shore of the bay was covered with people, and hundreds were swimming around the ships like shoals of fish." The Hawaiians held great feasts for the visitors, without expecting anything in return for their hospitality.

After a time, however, the Hawaiians grew impatient with Cook's men. The British broke many kapus and took objects from sacred temples. Though Cook is considered one of the more enlightened explorers, he and his men killed several Hawaiians. He also con-

The Hawaiians showered Captain Cook with hospitality, offering him gifts and holding elaborate feasts in his honor.

tinued to demand that the islanders provide food and supplies for his voyage.

The Hawaiians had had enough of these visitors. Lieutenant James King, one of Cook's crew, commented that the Hawaiians grew "very inquisitive about our time of departure." John Ledyard, another crewman, confirmed that the British had worn out their welcome. "It was also equally evident from the looks of the natives," Ledyard wrote, that "our former friendship was at an end, and that we had nothing to do but hasten our departure to some

LONO AND CAPTAIN COOK

One of the four main gods in the religion of the original Hawaiians was Lono, the god of rain, wind, fertility, and peace. According to legend, Lono killed his wife, Kaikilani, when he mistakenly suspected her of infidelity with a Hawaiian chief. In grief, he left in a large canoe with a tall mast and sails, promising one day to return on a floating island covered with trees. The Polynesians honored Lono with an annual harvest festival called the *makahiki*, which lasted from October to February. During this time war among the various tribes was suspended, and the people participated in canoe racing, surfing competitions, and other games.

When Captain Cook arrived in Hawaii in 1778, it was during the makahiki festival. Since he came in a boat with a tall mast and large sails, some Hawaiians assumed that he was the god Lono returning home. He had even arrived from the direction that the legend had predicted. This accounts for the hospitality shown him by the Hawaiians. Captain Cook's behavior eventually proved him less than a god. And after an English sailor shot a Hawaiian chief, Hawaiian warriors proved Cook mortal, stabbing and clubbing him to death.

different island where our vices were not known."

One day, Captain Cook became angry over the theft of one of the *Discovery*'s small boats. He went ashore planning to kidnap the king and hold him hostage until the boat was returned. As Cook escorted the king to the beach, the large crowd of Hawaiians who had gathered grew angry. A fight broke out, and Cook was slain. His shocked men sailed away.

THE HAOLE INVASION

From that time on, ships from England, France, Spain, the United States, and Russia made frequent stops in the Hawaiian Islands to rest and trade for fresh water, tropical fruits, fresh meat and fish, and such prized commodities as sandalwood, a rare fragrant wood. Hawaii lay right on the trade route that had sprung up across the Pacific: Pelts and furs were sent from Alaska and the Pacific Northwest to China, where they were exchanged for tea, silk, and porcelain. Soon, small communities of Europeans—merchants, traders, and farmers—were established on the islands.

Meanwhile, the chiefs of various islands had been at war with one another for control of Hawaii. Finally, in 1795, having defeated the last of his enemies and conquered all the other islands, King Kamehameha became the first ruler of a united Hawaiian kingdom. He proclaimed himself Kamehameha I.

Kamehameha died in 1819. From his deathbed he implored the native islanders to keep their traditions and "enjoy what I have made right." But his son, Liholiho, also known as Kamehameha II, had other ideas. He abolished the elaborate system of kapus,

Kamehameha I was the first king to rule over all the Hawaiian Islands.

which had made life so difficult for the common people. Though women were not supposed to eat with men, one day Liholiho sat down alongside his wife at an elaborate feast. With this simple act, the six-hundred-year-old kapu system was dead.

With the abandonment of the kapu system, the Polynesians were left with no religion. They began listening to the Protestant missionaries, who were trying to bring Christianity to the islands. Liholiho's successor, King Kamehameha III, passed laws against working on Sundays.

The missionaries built churches and established schools. By 1831, there were more than fifty thousand Hawaiians studying Western culture in Christian schools. The Protestant missionaries taught the Hawaiians that their heroic ancestors were primitive and sinful pagans. Too often, the price of Western education was a loss

LITTLE MOHEE

Nineteenth-century whalers often sailed south to Maui on their homeward voyage after a season of hunting their prey in the frigid Arctic waters. The woman in this song was a native of Maui, pronounced "Mohee" by the sailors.

As I went out walk-ing_____ up - on a fine day,_____

I got aw-ful lone-some_____ as the day passed a - way._____

_____ I sat down a - mus - ing_____ a - lone on the grass,

When who should sit by me,———— But a sweet In-dian lass.————

She sat down beside me upon a fine day,
I got awful lonesome as the day passed away,
She asked me to marry, and gave me her hand,
Said, "My pappy's a chieftain all over this land."

"My pappy's a chieftain and ruler be he,
I'm his only daughter and my name is Mohee."
I answered and told her that it never could be,
'Cause I had my own sweetheart in my own country.

I had my own sweetheart and I knew she loved me.
Her heart was as true as any Mohee.
So I said, "I must leave you and goodbye my dear,
There's a wind in my canvas and home I must steer."

At home with relations I tried for to see,
But there wasn't one there like my little Mohee;
And the girl I had trusted proved untrue to me,
So I sailed o'er the ocean to my little Mohee.

In the 1820s, missionaries came to the islands to convert the Hawaiians to Christianity.

of self-respect for the Hawaiians. A frequent visitor to the islands, Russian explorer Otto von Kotzebue, found Hawaii much changed by the missionaries. "The streets, formerly so full of life and animation, are now deserted," Kotzebue wrote. "Games of all kinds, even the most innocent, are sternly prohibited; singing is a punishable offense; and . . . attempting to dance would certainly find no mercy."

KING SUGAR

By the 1840s, Western influence was strong throughout the islands. The port cities of Honolulu, Hilo, and Lahaina had become bustling centers of commerce with the freewheeling atmosphere of American frontier towns. Honolulu had six hundred permanent European and American residents, and thousands of sailors from many nations took their liberty on the islands.

In 1833, a group of Boston merchants, Ladd & Company, had opened a large trading house in Honolulu. One of the firm's partners, William Hooper, purchased land on Kauai and began growing sugarcane. He built a mill to grind the cane stalks and press out their juice; then the liquid sugar was boiled into molasses and sugar crystals. Hooper's plantation was the beginning of what would become Hawaii's major industry in the second half of the nineteenth century.

By the mid-19th century, Honolulu had become a bustling trading center. Hawaii would eventually become known as the Crossroads of the Pacific.

Sugar was Hawaii's leading agricultural export by the mid-1800s. But the plantation owners faced a serious problem: They could not find enough laborers among the Hawaiians to harvest the cane. At the time of Captain Cook's visit, more than three hundred thousand people lived in Hawaii. By 1853, the number of native Hawaiians, called *kanakas*, had dwindled to around seventy thousand. Many had died of diseases introduced by the foreigners. Some young men had left the islands, seeking adventure by becoming sailors aboard foreign ships. Many who remained simply refused to work under the harsh conditions in the cane fields.

The planters solved their problem by bringing in workers from other nations. They looked to Asia for contract workers, people who, in exchange for free passage to Hawaii, promised to labor in the cane fields for three to five years. They received wages of a few dollars a day, shelter, food, and medical care. After their contract period was up, they were free to do as they pleased.

At first the planters brought in Chinese workers, then East Indians and Japanese, and then Koreans and Filipinos. Between 1850 and 1920, more than three hundred thousand immigrants from various parts of Asia arrived to seek their fortunes in the cane fields of Hawaii.

At the beginning of that period, people of Polynesian heritage made up more than 90 percent of the population of the Hawaiian Islands. By the end of it, Polynesians represented only 16 percent of the population, and Caucasians, less than 8 percent. People of Asian descent made up a great majority of the island's population—62 percent. They had become the new Hawaiians.

During the second half of the nineteenth century, Hawaiian

The owners of sugar plantations enticed hundreds of thousands of Asians to move to Hawaii to work in the cane fields. Here, Japanese laborers pose in front of their huts on the plantation.

society was transformed. The traditional Hawaiian community and its culture were destroyed. But a new, vibrant, multicultural community that makes Hawaii unique among the fifty states was born. The single greatest force driving this change was "King Sugar." "The farms where [the workers] have lived in close communities of many thousands have turned into towns as racially cosmopolitan as any in the world," wrote historian John W. Vandercook. "It is by no means the least of the sugar industry's accomplishments that in such towns the various groups live amiably together."

FROM KINGDOM TO STATE

Throughout the nineteenth century, the haole population was on the rise. Many of these whites were rich merchants, traders, and plantation owners. Since the taxes on their businesses paid for the Hawaiian government, they had a powerful influence on the monarchy. Some became the king's closest advisers.

With exposure to Western ideas of democracy came efforts by Hawaiians to reform the monarchy and limit its powers. In 1840, Kamehameha III announced a new written constitution that gave many powers to an elected legislature. Traditionally, all the land in the islands was owned by the king and the noble families. Then, in 1848, the king initiated the Great Mahele, a land-reform program that permitted individual ownership of private property and granted thousands of acres to commoners.

These reforms did not please all Hawaiians. The powers of the king had been reduced, but the legislature could be manipulated by the haoles to serve their business interests. Even the land-reform program made it much easier for foreigners to buy and control large tracts of land for sugar and pineapple plantations. The foreigners had nearly all the cash and could outbid small Hawaiian farmers for parcels of land. By about 1870, non-Hawaiians owned around 80 percent of the privately held land on the islands.

When King Kamehameha V died in 1872 without an heir, the dynasty died with him. From that point on, Hawaii's kings were elected. The first was King Lunalilo, whose cabinet was made up mostly of Americans.

Native islanders' fears of American influence had come true.

American businessmen compelled the king to sign a treaty with the United States to reduce tariffs (taxes on imports or exports) so that goods could be traded more freely and cheaply. In 1887, the haoles forced King David Kalakaua to agree to the "Bayonet Constitution," which restricted the vote to property owners, thus denying the vote to poorer Hawaiians who had no land.

When King Kalakaua died in 1891, he was succeeded by his sister, Queen Liliuokalani, a forceful woman who planned to change the constitution so that the monarchy would regain its power and foreign domination would be limited. Two years later, haole businessmen and sugar planters, aided by American troops, stormed the royal palace and overthrew the queen. By 1894 they had established a provisional government with the American

Queen Liliuokalani tried to resist the American takeover of Hawaii through nonviolent means. Although she failed, to this day her statue outside Iolani Palace is draped with fresh leis.

QUEEN LILIUOKALANI

Lydia Kamakaeha Paki became Queen Liliuokalani in 1891 when her brother, King David Kalakaua, died. As a child, she had been well schooled in poetry and music, and she later wrote "Aloha Oe," the most famous Hawaiian song. She came to the throne as a mature woman in her fifties, with the belief that preserving the Hawaiian monarchy was the only way to preserve the Hawaiian way of life. She was determined to take back some of the power her brother had surrendered to Western business interests.

When the queen announced that she wanted a new constitution in which more power was given to native Hawaiians and to the monarchy, even her own advisers deserted her. A delegation of influential haole citizens asked the United States minister to Hawaii, John L. Stevens, to protect their lives and property. On January 16, 1893, Stevens ordered marines from the visiting warship USS *Boston* to go ashore.

Queen Liliuokalani was arrested, charged with treason, and confined to Iolani Palace for nine months. A new republic was proclaimed in 1894 with a missionary's son, Sanford Dole, as president. The queen died in 1917, having spent her remaining years in her husband's house one block away from the palace. Liliuokalani was the first Hawaiian queen and the last Hawaiian monarch.

Sanford Dole as its president. Dole declared Hawaii a republic. President Grover Cleveland was embarrassed by this turn of events. "As I look back upon the first steps in this miserable business, and as I contemplate the means used to complete the outrage, I am ashamed of the whole affair," he said.

In 1898, after much urging by the haole community, the U.S.

Congress passed a resolution annexing Hawaii. Hawaiians were now American citizens, but they had no official representation in the federal government in Washington. Many Hawaiians continued to resent the sugar growers, whose power had only increased. "Sugar is King in Hawaii to a far greater extent than cotton was in the Old South," journalist Ray Stannard Balzer wrote after visiting the islands in 1911. "Those rich, warm lands in all the islands are devoted almost exclusively now to the production of sugar cane."

Some islanders began to work for statehood, but many people on the mainland resisted. Some argued against granting Hawaii statehood because they believed that its Asian communities were alien to the United States and its way of life. Attitudes began to change when the Japanese attacked the naval base at Pearl Harbor on December 7, 1941. With this surprise raid, Hawaiians became the only Americans to suffer an attack by a foreign power in this century. Americans saw Hawaiians of all backgrounds pull together to help the United States defeat Japan and win the war.

Though they were intensely loyal to the United States, Japanese Americans in Hawaii suffered a great deal of discrimination during World War II. There were too many of them on the islands to place them in internment camps, as was done on the mainland, but their activities were restricted and watched. To be treated with such suspicion hurt the Japanese on the islands. "Hawaii is our home; the United States, our country. We know but one loyalty and that is to the Stars and Stripes. We wish to do our part as loyal Americans in every way possible, and we hereby offer ourselves for whatever service you may see fit to use us," stated 150 Hawaiians of Japanese descent after they were dismissed from the Hawaii

Japanese Americans joined the U.S. armed forces by the thousands after America entered World War II. Here, 2,645 young enlistees prepare to leave Honolulu to fight the war.

Territorial Guard following the attack on Pearl Harbor.

Young Japanese Americans volunteered in great numbers to serve in the United States armed forces. One fighting unit, the 442nd Regimental Combat Team, was composed entirely of Japanese Americans and became the most decorated group of soldiers in the entire American army. "You fought not only the enemy but you fought prejudice—and you have won," President Harry S. Truman told the proud men of the 442nd as he honored them in Washington, D.C., after the war.

The push for statehood eventually succeeded: Hawaii became the fiftieth state in 1959. In the years since, this colorful society, with its many cultures and traditions, has become a model for how Americans of different backgrounds can live together and prosper.

The Honolulu Star-Bulletin *celebrates Hawaii's admission as the fiftieth state.*

3 WORKING IN THE ISLANDS

The capitol in Honolulu

Hawaii's economy is usually very strong, but it is also very dependent on one industry—tourism. As a result, the state government has to carefully balance the need to encourage tourism and development with its people's desire to maintain their unique way of life.

INSIDE GOVERNMENT

Like most states, Hawaii's state government is divided into three branches: executive, legislative, and judicial.

Executive. The executive branch is headed by the governor, who is elected for a four-year term. The governor can recommend legislation and veto (reject) bills passed by the legislature. The governor also appoints top officials such as attorney general, finance director, and judges. These positions are elective in most states, but in Hawaii, only the governor and the lieutenant governor are elected.

Benjamin J. Cayetano, who became governor in 1994, is the first Filipino-American governor of any state. He was born in Honolulu into a poor immigrant family. "I don't remember hardship," Cayetano once said, "but if you've never tasted steak, you never know what you're missing." Although Filipinos were discouraged from being anything but laborers, Cayetano went to college, became a lawyer, and entered politics. As governor, he has worked

Benjamin Cayetano is the country's first Filipino-American governor. "The genius of Hawaiian politics is that nobody has fifty-one percent," says historian Dan Boylan. "If you want to win you have to cross ethnic lines."

hard to promote Hawaii's interests during a difficult economic period. He once said, "When you're an elected official, you're given a great privilege and a great burden. You need to feel a sense of urgency about what you do."

John Waihee, who served from 1986 to 1994, was the first Hawaiian of Polynesian ancestry to be governor. During his tenure, Hawaii became the first state in the Union to adopt universal health care. He also was known for promoting cooperation between government and private landowners in trying to protect Hawaii's delicate environment.

Legislative. The Hawaiian legislature is composed of a senate, with twenty-five members elected for four-year terms, and a house of representatives, with fifty-one members elected for two-year terms. A majority vote in both the house and senate is required to pass a bill, which is then sent to the governor to be signed into law. The legislature can override the governor's vetoes if two-thirds of the members agree. The senate also approves the appointments made by the governor.

Judicial. The role of the Hawaiian court system is to administer justice impartially. Hawaii has many district and circuit courts and a family court. If someone disagrees with a decision made by these courts, they can ask the intermediate court of appeals to overturn the

John Waihee, the first native governor of Hawaii

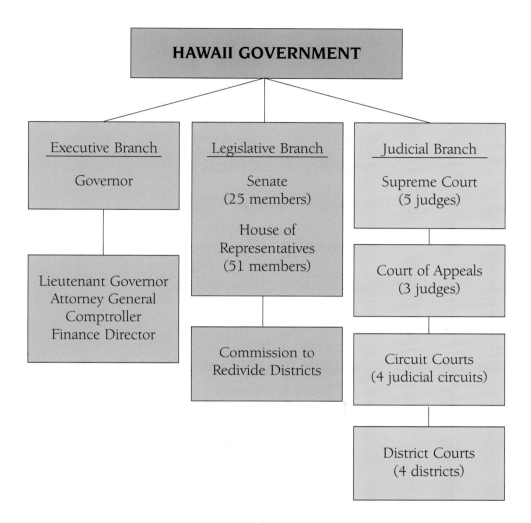

HAWAII GOVERNMENT

Executive Branch

Governor

Lieutenant Governor
Attorney General
Comptroller
Finance Director

Legislative Branch

Senate
(25 members)

House of
Representatives
(51 members)

Commission to
Redivide Districts

Judicial Branch

Supreme Court
(5 judges)

Court of Appeals
(3 judges)

Circuit Courts
(4 judicial circuits)

District Courts
(4 districts)

ruling. Further appeals can be taken to the state supreme court, the highest court in Hawaii.

Local government. Hawaii is unusual in that it has no city governments. The city of Honolulu is the state capital, but it is governed as part of Honolulu County, which includes the entire island of Oahu. Each county has a mayor and council. These county governments provide services such as police and firefighters, which cities provide in other states.

THE NATIVE SOVEREIGNTY MOVEMENT

Some native Hawaiians still question whether the islands should be part of the United States. They believe they should govern themselves. The native Hawaiian sovereignty movement is central to Hawaiian politics today.

Though only about nine thousand Hawaiians can claim pure Hawaiian ancestry, there are about two hundred thousand people who are partly native Hawaiian. They call themselves the *kanaka maoli*. As a group they have the lowest income, the shortest life expectancy, the highest rate of infant mortality, and the lowest level of education.

In the fall of 1993, the United States Congress passed the so-called Apology Resolution, which President Bill Clinton signed into law. The resolution formally acknowledged that the overthrow of Queen Liliuokalani and the Hawaiian monarchy in 1893 by American businessmen and U.S. Marines was illegal.

Lilikala Kame'eleihiwa, who teaches Hawaiian studies at the University of Hawaii, summed up the attitude of many kanaka maoli when she said, "We are an occupied people." Although some people liken the situation of the native Hawaiians to that of Native Americans elsewhere in the United States, many native Hawaiians resent such comparisons. They point out that their heritage and history are unique. "First they made us Hawaiians, then they said we're Americans; now they want to make us Indian?" Michael Grace, a kanaka maoli activist, scornfully asks.

Many different groups have taken up the cause of Hawaiian sovereignty. In early 1994, a coalition of these groups met at Iolani

Iolani Palace, the 19th-century home of the Hawaiian monarchy, has great symbolic value to groups working for Hawaiian sovereignty.

Palace, the royal palace of the Hawaiian monarchy, and issued the Proclamation of Restoration of Independence of the Sovereign Nation State of Hawaii. By early 1995, they had agreed on a new constitution for their nation. Though none of these documents have the force of law, they have caused a great deal of political controversy.

Native Hawaiian groups disagree about what kind of independence they should have. Some think they should have a nation within a nation, similar to an Indian reservation. Others are demanding reparations and the return of the lands held in trust for them by the state and federal governments. Much of that land has been developed as state parks, private farms and ranches, and beachfront resorts, so many complications would arise. Still other kanaka maoli groups are demanding complete independence, restoration of the Hawaiian monarchy, restrictions on the immigration of non-Hawaiians, and the denial of voting rights to non-Hawaiian residents. Recent polls have shown that 75 percent of all Hawaiian residents would support some type of greater autonomy for native Hawaiians if union with the United States were not lost.

TODAY'S CONCERNS

Like Americans everywhere, Hawaiians worry about whether their economy will remain strong enough to provide well-paid jobs for the state's citizens and a bright future for its children. For the past several decades, Hawaii has been one of the nation's most prosperous states. Average income in Hawaii is higher than the national average, and the unemployment rate is consistently lower than the national average. The state also ranks high in the amount of money spent on public education.

Hawaii is growing more urban, and big-city problems such as crime are on the rise. A visitor to Hawaii might be surprised to learn that the crime rate on this island paradise is higher than the national average. Most of Hawaii's crimes, though, are nonviolent offenses such as burglary and theft. The rate of violent crime is among the lowest in the country. Still, in recent years the numbers of such crimes have risen, reminding Hawaiians of how difficult it is to maintain the quality of life that makes their state so special.

Another urban problem that plagues Hawaiians is miserable traffic. Many people who live in Honolulu's outskirts have gotten used to eating their breakfast while they crawl along at fifteen miles per hour during their ninety-minute morning commute. Gina Hirata used to leave home at 5:30 A.M. to beat the traffic. She got into Honolulu by 6:30, an hour and a half before she was supposed to be at work. "I didn't want to deal with the traffic, so I just sort of sat in my car and rested until it was time to go into my job," she said. "It was kind of ridiculous." Now she has a job in the suburbs, twenty minutes from her home.

No one has figured out how to solve the problem. The number of cars keeps rising, and all of Oahu between the mountains and the beach is developed, so there is nowhere to build new highways. "We're pretty much resigned to the fact that state engineers are never going to solve the traffic problems," says David Nagata, who drives into Honolulu from Pearl Harbor every day. "This is a very

EARNING A LIVING

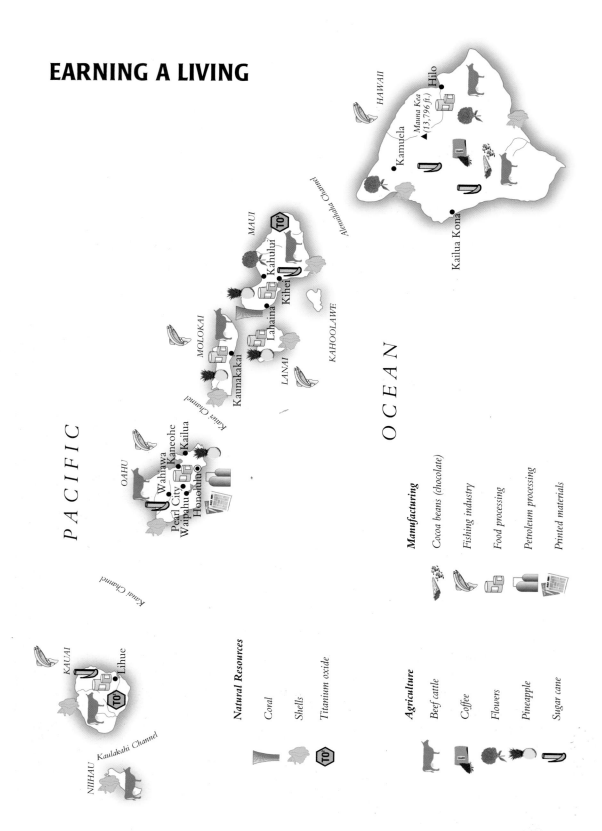

PACIFIC

OCEAN

HAWAII
Hilo
Mauna Kea
(13,796 ft.)
Kamuela
Kailua Kona

MAUI
Kahului
Kiihei
Lahaina

MOLOKAI
Kaunakakai

LANAI

KAHOOLAWE

Alenuihaha Channel

Kalui Channel

OAHU
Wahiawa
Kaneohe
Kailua
Pearl City
Waipahu
Honolulu

Kauai Channel

KAUAI
Lihue

NIIHAU

Kaulakahi Channel

Natural Resources

Coral

Shells

Titanium oxide

Manufacturing

Cocoa beans (chocolate)

Fishing industry

Food processing

Petroleum processing

Printed materials

Agriculture

Beef cattle

Coffee

Flowers

Pineapple

Sugar cane

small island for the amount of people who live here, and there are no limits on the amount of cars. Traffic is a way of life on Oahu." But he has no intention of moving. "I like the life here," he says.

THE HIGH PRICE OF PARADISE

Some of the factors that make Hawaii special also give it special problems. As an island state several thousand miles off the American mainland, Hawaii must import many items, from automobiles

Because of its distance from the U.S. mainland, Hawaii has to import many goods, resulting in busy ports but high prices.

to building materials to food and clothing. This makes for a higher-than-usual cost of living in the state. In fact, the cost of living is 40 percent higher than the national average, while the average income is only 10 percent higher.

The state's natural beauty also indirectly contributes to the high cost of living. Hawaiians are very concerned with preserving their landscape, and a huge percentage of the state's land is owned or maintained by the government. That makes available land very expensive. In the 1980s, there was also a huge amount of resort and hotel development. As investors bought up land like mad, housing prices skyrocketed, doubling between 1986 and 1990. Hawaii now has some of the highest-priced real estate in the world.

Often, people have to work two or three jobs just to make ends meet. Maria Naehu and her husband live on Oahu and together make ninety thousand dollars a year. They want to have children and own a single-family house, but feel that they can't afford both. "All our friends are in the same boat," she says. "We constantly sit around and anguish over whether we should stay here or make the break."

Many people further down the economic scale don't have any choice. All four of Edwena Kamohalii's siblings have had to leave Hawaii. "The cost of living in Hawaii is outrageous," she says. "You're not going to make it flipping burgers at Burger King."

HAWAII TODAY AND TOMORROW

New business opportunities and an inviting climate caused the population of Hawaii to grow quickly in the late twentieth

1992 GROSS STATE PRODUCT: $33 BILLION

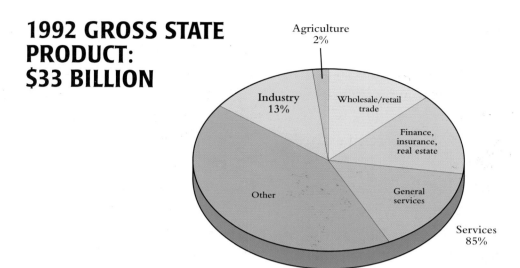

Agriculture
2%

Industry
13%

Wholesale/retail
trade

Finance,
insurance,
real estate

Other

General
services

Services
85%

century. Tourism changed the face of Hawaii as millions of jet-age travelers began to discover the islands' magnificent beaches and scenery. It is now the state's largest industry and accounts for more than 30 percent of its income. Every year, more than six million visitors go to the islands and spend $10 billion.

The second-largest sector of the economy is the United States military, which contributes about $3 billion to the state annually. The military supports more than fifty thousand soldiers and sailors who are stationed in Hawaii, almost twenty thousand civilian workers, and about sixty thousand dependents of military personnel. In no other state do armed-forces personnel and their families make up such a large percentage of the population. Changes in the nation's military policy often directly affect Hawaiians, because any reduction in military spending can hurt the Hawaiian economy.

Though agriculture no longer dominates, it is still the third-largest contributor to the Hawaiian economy. The state's major

The U.S. military is vital to the Hawaiian economy.

Cut flowers, like these anthuriums, are among the many products exported by Hawaii.

exports are sugar, pineapples, cattle, coffee, papayas, and cut flowers. Hawaii is also the world's largest producer of macadamia nuts. The once mighty sugar industry, although still important, has been humbled. After decades of labor struggles, the men and women who work in the cane fields have become highly paid workers. As a result, sugarcane production has been slowly shifting to low-wage countries such as the Philippines and Taiwan.

During the 1970s and 1980s, the Japanese purchased a great deal of real estate in Hawaii. Although that created an economic boom, some Hawaiians were ambivalent about it. "The immediate effect of Japanese hotel development on Maui was the increased urbanization of our shorelines and loss of open beaches," says Maui resident Dana Noane Hall. She believes that many Hawaiians "feel trapped by having to support an industry that may give them a job but that takes away from their ability to enjoy the place they live— to dive, to fish, to swim. Instead, they get to look at a glossy brochure of out-of-state residents doing what they used to do."

A recession in the early 1990s in Japan reduced Japanese investment and hurt the Hawaiian economy. Japanese tourism was also affected by the recession, and Hawaii felt the pinch. In 1995, Governor Cayetano called for a reduction in government spending on social programs and a new emphasis on tourism and high-technology industry to stimulate the economy. Despite the difficulties, Cayetano was optimistic about Hawaii's economic future. "Recently, a friend told me that this is a terrible time to be governor," he said, "that there was no money to do anything and that he felt sorry for me. I disagree with him."

4 HAWAIIAN STYLE

Who are the real Hawaiians? Hawaiians have worked out their own answer to this difficult question. As Hawaiian businessman George Kanakele explains, "These days, any resident of this state who considers Hawaii his home and who has an understanding of the values of Hawaiian culture ought to consider himself or herself a Hawaiian."

Hawaiians live their lives and go about their daily work in much the same way as other Americans. Nevertheless, this remote group of tropical islands, with its mix of Polynesian, Asian, and Western peoples, has its own unique culture and style of living.

THE ALOHA SPIRIT

The first difference visitors notice when they arrive in Hawaii is the warm spirit of greeting extended to strangers. This is the spirit of aloha, or welcome, which is symbolized by the lei, the necklace woven of flowers that is given to every visitor upon arrival. There are many kinds of leis, made of different flowers, berries, nuts, ferns, vines, leaves, shells, and even bird feathers. In Polynesian times, the lei was used as an offering to the gods in sacred rituals and dances. Each island has its own style of lei-making and its own combination of materials. The most prized is the shell lei from

Hawaii's spirit of aloha is symbolized by the lei. These beautiful flower wreaths can be worn as necklaces or headbands.

Niihau, which is more likely to be found in expensive jewelry shops and craft galleries than around the necks of visitors.

THE LUAU

The most famous Hawaiian ritual is the luau, a great feast staged to celebrate weddings, christenings, birthdays, and other important events. Nowadays, tourists can experience a commercialized

Roast pig is the centerpiece of most luaus.

version of the luau at almost any Hawaiian hotel, but the traditional celebration involved family and friends and brought everyone together for several days to prepare the food and enjoy the festive activities. The meal can be eaten indoors or outdoors. It lasts for the entire evening, as a huge display of food is laid out before the guests on a bed of banana leaves or bamboo mats.

The main dish is usually pig, which is wrapped in ti leaves and roasted in an *imu*, an earthen pit filled with kiawe wood and hot

MACADAMIA NUT BISCUITS

Hawaii is renowned for its macadamia nuts. Adding them to recipes is an easy way to make regular food a little bit special. Have an adult help you with this recipe.

- 2 cups flour
- 1 cup soft butter
- ½ cup brown sugar
- 1 teaspoon grated orange peel
- 1 cup chopped macadamia nuts

Mix the flour, butter, sugar, and orange peel until the batter is smooth. Stir in the nuts. Chill the dough for half an hour. Put the dough between pieces of wax paper and roll it out until it is about ¼ inch thick. Cut the dough into 2-inch squares and place 1½ inches apart on a cookie sheet. Bake at 325 degrees for about 20 minutes. The biscuits are done when they're golden.

lava stones. The pig is surrounded by fish, taro, breadfruit, squid, and yams, and the rest of the table is laid out with the many fruits native to the islands—papayas, mangoes, guavas, passion fruit, litchis, kumquats, tamarinds, and pineapples. Fish dishes may include salmon, red snapper, or yellowfin tuna. There also might be octopus, prawns, lobsters, or shrimp.

The taro root produces another popular Hawaiian dish certain to be served at luaus. This is poi. The taro is baked, mashed to a pulp, strained, and eaten as a gray paste. It is a starchy food that takes the place of potatoes or bread in the European diet. It is often eaten out of a calabash shell. The feast usually concludes with a dessert of haupia, a coconut pudding.

MUSIC AND DANCE

With its dreamy melodies and lyrics, Hawaiian music is immensely popular. The most famous musical instrument, the ukulele, evolved from the *machete*, a type of guitar first brought to the islands by Portuguese who immigrated to work in the cane fields. In Hawaiian, *ukulele* means "jumping flea," a colorful description of how the instrument sounds.

Other unique musical instruments are the *kalaau*, wooden sticks that produce the tone of a xylophone; the *ili ili*, stone castanets; the *pu ili*, split bamboo sticks; and the *ipu*, a series of hollow gourds. The steel guitar is also an essential part of any Hawaiian ensemble. It was invented by Joseph Kekuku in the 1880s. What gives much Hawaiian music its unique sound is the slack-key style of playing, in which the strings of certain instruments are loosened and played off-key.

Although many unusual instruments are important to Hawaiian music, the ukulele is the most famous.

The dance most closely associated with Hawaiian music is the hula. It is a traditional Hawaiian folk dance, performed in ancient times in worship of Laka, the sister of the fire goddess, Pele. Early in Polynesian history, the hula was danced only by men in religious ceremonies. It required a great deal of training and practice to master the more than two hundred dances and their accompanying chants.

As men became more preoccupied with making war, women

took over the hula traditions. The first missionaries disapproved of the hula because they thought it was too provocative, and for a time they succeeded in preventing its performance. The dance was revived by King David Kalakaua. Today, it thrives as a popular commercial entertainment and as a serious art form performed in the traditional manner by a small group of Hawaiian dancers who are interested in preserving the old culture. Hula schools and *kuma hula*, or hula masters, are coming back into fashion.

Carrying on the traditions of their ancestors, many young Hawaiians learn to dance the hula.

In the nineteenth century, Hawaiian royalty had a profound impact on the islanders' music. In 1868, King Kamehameha V established the Royal Hawaiian Band and hired Heinrich (Henry) Berger to lead it. The German bandmaster became known as the father of Hawaiian music. In his forty-odd years as bandleader, he arranged more than one thousand Hawaiian songs for performance, composed seventy-five original songs, and conducted more than thirty thousand concerts. The Royal Hawaiian Band still performs public concerts every week near Iolani Palace.

Besides reviving hula dancing, King David Kalakaua also cowrote, with Heinrich Berger, Hawaii's anthem, "Hawaii Ponoi." His sister, Queen Liliuokalani, wrote the most famous Hawaiian song of all, "Aloha Oe." From the 1930s to the 1960s, Hawaiian music, or a Western imitation of it, was popular throughout the world. It, in turn, absorbed influences from jazz, ragtime, blues, and Latin music.

Today, rock and roll has captured the imagination of many Hawaiian performers. But there are also young musicians, part of a growing movement of culturally conscious people, who compose and perform in traditional styles.

SPEAKING HAWAIIAN

Although the Hawaiian language is taught in some high schools and universities, no more than two thousand residents of the island still speak it fluently, and they are mostly older people. Despite efforts to preserve it, Hawaiian is probably on its way to extinction as a living, spoken language.

THE HAWAIIAN SHIRT

That bright, flashy, outrageously colored shirt known as the Hawaiian or aloha shirt got its start in the 1930s, when the Hawaiian garment industry stopped producing only tough, practical clothing for the plantation workers. Sport shirts made of Japanese kimono fabric were popular among schoolchildren: bright oranges and pinks for the girls, bold blues and browns for the boys. Hawaiian designers were soon creating new Hawaiian patterns—ukuleles and leis, surfboards and palm trees, cliff and beach scenes—and distinctively splashy patterns of color.

The market for the aloha shirt eventually shifted to adults, at first to tourists. By the end of World War II, even the locals were wearing them. In 1947, Honolulu County employees were allowed to wear Hawaiian shirts during the summer, and by 1970, these shirts had practically replaced the business suit on the islands.

The Hawaiian shirt eventually even caught on in the continental United States. It reached its peak popularity in the 1950s thanks to film and television stars such as Elvis Presley and Arthur Godfrey. But fashions change. By the late 1970s, many people thought the shirts were too corny to wear anywhere except in Hawaii, and production fell off. But some diehards wear them still.

The Hawaiian language has contributed many words to the vocabulary of the islanders. The most famous is "aloha."

The ancient Hawaiians had no alphabet. In the early 1820s, Protestant missionaries devised a written alphabet for the Hawaiian language as part of their efforts to Christianize the Polynesians. It has only twelve letters, the consonants *h, k, l, m, n, p,* and *w,* and the vowels *a, e, i, o,* and *u.* An apostrophe is sometimes included in the written form of words to indicate a brief, silent pause.

Today, the English language is dominant in the state, though the state's native language has contributed hundreds of words to the everyday speech of all Hawaiians and helps maintain the special character of the islands' culture. Some Hawaiians who don't speak English well speak a kind of pidgin English instead, using words from English, Hawaiian, and the many other languages of this multiethnic society.

RIDING THE WAVES

Although Hawaiians enjoy many different sports, there is one that they can justly claim to have originated—the ancient sport of *heenalu*, or surfing. Surfing is mentioned in Hawaiian songs dating back to the fifteenth century. When Captain Cook arrived in 1778, his men marveled at how the Polynesians seemed to glide so effortlessly on the powerful, rolling waves.

Tourists and locals alike enjoy riding Hawaii's fantastic waves.

In those days, the Hawaiian nobility used sixteen-foot boards weighing as much as one hundred fifty pounds, and many of the best surfing beaches were reserved exclusively for their use. The commoners used shorter boards, which were about six feet long. After watching these men ride the waves, Mark Twain observed that ". . . it did not seem that a lightning express train could shoot along at a more hair-lifting speed."

The missionaries discouraged surfing, and interest in the sport waned as the native population declined and their way of life became more westernized. Then in the early twentieth century, Hawaiians revived the sport. Today's surfboards are smaller and lighter and are often made of synthetic materials. The most famous surfing competitions occur during the winter along the northern shores of Oahu, where the waves are incredible.

MANY HAWAIIS

People from more than fifty different ethnic groups are found in the Hawaiian Islands. These include Japanese, Chinese, Koreans, Filipinos, Samoans, Portuguese, Spaniards, Italians, Germans, Norwegians, Russians, English, Scots, Puerto Ricans, and native Hawaiians. The strong Asian and Polynesian influence make Hawaii unique among American states.

About a third of the population has mixed ancestry, and the number is increasing. Six out of every ten children born in the islands are of mixed blood. Hawaii is, in fact, the most racially integrated state in the Union. Many people believe that is why Hawaii has fewer racial problems than other states. "Everybody's

ETHNIC HAWAII

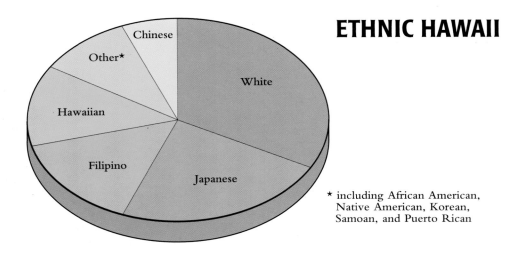

* including African American, Native American, Korean, Samoan, and Puerto Rican

got a Japanese daughter-in-law or a Chinese son-in-law or a Filipino relative," says David A. Heenan, a white businessman whose wife is Filipino. "It's hard to throw stones at somebody when they're in the family." In Hawaii, there is no majority ethnic group; every group is a minority.

Of the more than 1 million people on the islands, about 240,000—almost 25 percent of the state's population—are of Japanese descent. The first Japanese began to arrive in 1868, when Japan was suffering economic upheaval. They called Hawaii *Tenjiku*, the "heavenly place." By 1900, with a population of 60,000, they were already the largest ethnic group in Hawaii.

Today, the Japanese-American community is very successful in business and government. They celebrate their heritage several times during the year, beginning in March with Girls' Day. On that day, it is customary to give young girls a doll, and the department stores are full of doll displays. During the eleven-week Cherry Blossom Festival, there are demonstrations of the tea ceremony,

Japanese Americans are the largest ethnic group in Hawaii. Many are successful in business and government.

martial arts, flower arranging, and bonsai gardening, and a cherry blossom queen is crowned. When Boys' Day is celebrated on May 5, the sky is filled with color. Paper carps are flown from rooftops as symbols of strength and courage, and families fly a special kite for each son.

The Chinese began arriving in Hawaii in great numbers in the 1850s, when the sugar growers started importing labor from Asia. The Chinese called Hawaii *Tan Hueng Shan*, "land of the fragrant

The finishing touches are put on an elaborate kite that will fly above the rooftops on Boys' Day.

hills," after the pleasing aroma of the sandalwood trees that are now so rare.

About sixty thousand Chinese Americans now live in Hawaii, mostly on the island of Oahu. Sometime in late January, the Chinese New Year is celebrated. At this time, the streets are filled with the sounds of exploding firecrackers, and huge paper lions snake their way through the streets, scaring away the bad spirits.

The Chinese also celebrate Buddha's birthday in April with tea ceremonies and traditional singing and dancing.

About 140,000 Hawaiians are of Filipino ancestry. They came a little later than other groups, a few arriving in 1906, and a larger number after 1924. Many Filipinos were brought in as strikebreakers when earlier Chinese and Japanese immigrants began to demand higher wages from the plantation owners. At first, older immigrants were prejudiced against them. Although the Filipinos soon organized and began to agitate for improved working conditions on their own, they remain among the poorest groups in the

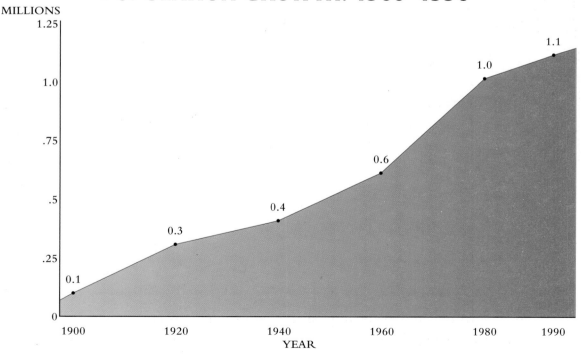

POPULATION GROWTH: 1900–1990

At the Polynesian Cultural Center, native Hawaiians proudly recall their heritage through such activities as canoe demonstrations.

state. In May, they hold the Fiesta Filipina, which includes traditional foods, music and dance, exhibitions of handicrafts, and a beauty contest.

Hawaii's small community of about twenty thousand Korean Americans has integrated into the larger society more than other groups have, and their rate of intermarriage is high. Koreans first came to Hawaii to work in the cane fields in the early 1900s.

Hawaiians of Polynesian ancestry hold their Merry Monarch Festival in April, honoring King David Kalakaua, who revived the hula and was renowned for his love of drinking and merrymaking. King Kamehameha Day on June 11 is a state holiday, as is Prince Kuhio Day on March 26. The fall brings Aloha Week, which features parades, pageants, balls, and the coronation of a royal court at Iolani Palace. *Na Mele o Maui* is a five-day festival during December that is devoted to Hawaiian culture. It features displays of native arts and crafts, canoe races, and luaus.

There are about 370,000 Caucasians in Hawaii, or about 33 percent of the population, the smallest percentage in any American state. Many are the descendants of European and American merchants, businesspeople, missionaries, sailors, and cane field workers. There are also many *malihini*, or newcomers—mainlanders who are drawn to the island state by its climate, scenery, and unique way of life.

Hawaii also has small communities of Samoans, Puerto Ricans, blacks, and Portuguese, all of whom have made contributions to the eclectic Hawaiian culture. This ethnic diversity is reflected in the language, food, and festivals that Hawaiians enjoy. To many visitors, Hawaii seems always in a festive mood.

5 STANDING OUT

Hawaiian Island pageant, Kamuela Ranch

Hawaii has many fine native sons and daughters who have made their mark on the world. Their stories are as varied as the state from which they come.

A FAVORITE POLITICIAN

Perhaps the most prominent Hawaiian in modern times is Senator Daniel K. Inouye. This Democratic senator has been one of the most skillful and respected leaders in Congress for more than thirty-five years. Inouye was born in Honolulu, one of four children of Japanese immigrants. The son of a department store clerk, he dreamed of becoming a doctor. But that hope was dashed by World War II.

After the Japanese attacked Pearl Harbor, many Japanese Americans, suffering prejudice and discrimination due to their ancestry, yearned to prove their loyalty to the United States. Inouye was no exception, and he joined the army soon after he graduated from high school.

Inouye volunteered for the 442nd Regimental Combat Team, the first all-Japanese-American combat unit, which became the most decorated unit in the history of the U.S. Army. Two days before the end of the war in Europe, Inouye led his platoon in an assault on a German infantry position. One arm was shattered by

Senator Daniel Inouye has been serving Hawaii as long as it has been a state.

an enemy rifle grenade, and he was shot in the stomach and the legs. Despite his wounds, he managed to hurl grenades that destroyed three German machine-gun sites, saving his platoon. For this and other acts of bravery, he received the Distinguished Service Cross, the Bronze Star, and the Purple Heart. Inouye's right arm had to be amputated, and he spent two years in army hospitals, recuperating from his wounds.

Afterward, Inouye went to college and became a lawyer. He was later elected to the territorial senate, and when Hawaii became a state in 1959, he was elected to the U.S. House of Representatives, becoming the first Japanese American ever to serve in Congress.

Three years later, he moved to the Senate, where he has remained ever since. Inouye is one of the most popular figures in the Senate. He has been a consistent supporter of civil rights legislation and an articulate spokesman for Asian Americans and all his fellow Hawaiians.

A HERO IN SPACE

One of the seven astronauts to die in the explosion of the space shuttle *Challenger* in 1986, Ellison Shoji Onizuka is a hero to many

Ellison Onizuka and his crewmates head to the Challenger *for its fateful flight.*

people across the nation. From childhood, Onizuka dreamed of traveling into space. He loved looking at the stars through telescopes and paid close attention to the careers of the first astronauts in the 1960s. "Ellison always had it in mind to become an astronaut," his brother recalled, "but he was too embarrassed to tell anyone. When he was growing up, there were no Asian astronauts, no black astronauts, just white ones. His dream seemed too big."

But it wasn't. Onizuka studied aerospace engineering in college, joined the air force, and entered the astronaut-training program. Aboard the space shuttle *Discovery* in January 1985, his dream came true. All at once, Onizuka became the first Japanese-American, first Hawaiian, and first Buddhist astronaut.

Onizuka was aware of the risks he undertook. After his *Discovery* flight, he told reporters, "You're really aware that you're on top of a monster; you're totally at the mercy of the vehicle." The *Challenger* accident immortalized him as an ordinary American willing to live with those risks.

ENTERTAINING THE WORLD

Say the words "Hawaiian entertainer" and many people envision someone in a splashy shirt singing "Aloha Oe." But Bette Midler, Hawaii's most famous performer, is known for her brassy sense of humor and her love of show tunes. Midler is the daughter of a house painter. She was born in Honolulu and grew up in a poor area amid sugarcane fields near Pearl Harbor. Coming from the only Jewish family in a neighborhood made up mostly of Chinese, Japanese, Samoans, and native Hawaiians, Bette often felt lonely

The Divine Miss M is always entertaining.

and out of place. She eventually found that performing helped. After falling in love with musicals, she took to belting out songs in the tin shower of her family's home, so everyone in the neighborhood could hear. "People used to gather outside to call up requests or yell that I was lousy," she recalled.

At nineteen, she landed a bit part in the film adaptation of James Michener's novel *Hawaii*. When the production returned to California, Midler went with it. Soon she was getting parts in plays and perfecting her outrageous nightclub act, calling herself the Divine Miss M. Today, she is one of America's favorite comediennes, entertaining people everywhere with such films as *First Wives Club* and *Ruthless People*.

THE HUMAN FISH

Many great surfers have hailed from Hawaii, where the sport was invented, but one name looms above all the others—Duke Kahanamoku. Duke grew up near Waikiki. He spent much of his

Duke Kahanamoku was renowned for his surfboard tricks. Here, he tees off from his board while cruising in on the breakers.

youth on the beach and in the waves, serving as a lifeguard and a surfing instructor. He entertained tourists and locals alike with his surfing tricks, such as riding backward, performing handstands, and even surfing with a dog sitting in front of him on the board. Perfecting these maneuvers that no one had ever done before earned him the title "the father of modern surfing."

Duke was also a great swimmer. At the 1912 Olympics in Stockholm, Sweden, he shattered the world record in the hundred-meter freestyle, beating the old record by three seconds. Some people started calling him the human fish. He won more medals in 1920 and 1924. In 1932, at age forty-two, Kahanamoku qualified for his final Olympics, making the water polo team. "I just wanted to see if I could still swim," he said. After he retired, he still had a long career ahead of him—as the sheriff of Honolulu, an elected position that he held for twenty-nine years.

TODAY'S VOICES

In the nineteenth century, many famous writers visited Hawaii and were enchanted by its charms. Herman Melville, Robert Louis Stevenson, and Mark Twain wrote lovingly of the tropical wonderland they had discovered. Today, many Hawaiians are telling their own stories, writing tales of the islands and their culture and what it is like to grow up in this multiethnic melting pot.

Honolulu native Cathy Song is one of the best young poets in America. Her poignant poems capture precise moments in her childhood and in her family's past. Another talented writer, Sylvia Watanabe, has produced a short-story collection called *Talking to the Dead*. These honest, affectionate stories tell about everyday life on Maui before it was overrun with tourists. "I wanted to record a way of life which I loved and which seemed in danger of dying away. . . . I wanted to tell how the Lahaina coast looked before it was covered with resorts," Watanabe once wrote. "I wanted to save my parents' and grandparents' stories."

Kathleen Tyau grew up on Oahu. Her funny, exuberant novel called *A Little Too Much Is Enough* concerns a family of Chinese

Novelist Kathleen Tyau

In the following excerpt from Kathleen Tyau's novel *A Little Too Much Is Enough*, fifteen-year-old Mahealani describes her first day working at the pineapple cannery.

and native Hawaiians during the decades following World War II. Tyau delights in describing food, from the details of making poi to the sensation of stuffing yourself at a nine-course wedding banquet. But while she revels in the pleasures of the islands, she doesn't shrink from portraying the darker side of life there, such as the horrible work in the pineapple canneries. She depicts Hawaiian life in all its joy and pain.

The women next to me are singing, but I don't know the words. I can hear only the chopping of the genakas and the grinding of the belts and the clanking of the cans. And the forelady shouts from behind, Pick up your pine, pick up your pine. Other hands reach for the pine, but not mine. I am trying to spin a whole pineapple on my thumb. The forelady yells, paces up and down, finally yanks me from my stool at the front of the line and moves me to the end of the row of trimmers. She points at a plastic tub. She makes the words big in her mouth: Fill. It. Up. I remove the pineapples from the belt that the trimmers have missed because they are one girl short, because of me. I grab the pineapples before they reach the slicing machine. Haul them to the front of the line where the faster trimmers trim. Eyes left and right flying off the pine. The girls are singing, knife blades flashing, and I am catching pine.

Pineapple twirling on thumbs, knives slashing, eyes falling into the trough, cans and belts clattering, banging. And the marching, pineapples marching down the line, from the trimmers to the slicing machine, from the slicer to the packers, from the packers to the can. And all the way down the line, the forelady cries, Pick up your pine, pick up your pine.

6 A TOUR OF THE ISLANDS

Six million visitors come to the Hawaiian Islands every year in search of warm, sunny beaches, dramatic scenery, and a slower pace of life. Hawaii is a paradise for lovers of the outdoors. There are magnificent opportunities for swimming, surfing, fishing, hiking, camping, scuba diving, rock climbing, horseback riding, and sailing.

HONOLULU

Most visitors to Hawaii today arrive by airplane at the international airport on the island of Oahu. There are about eighty thousand tourists on Oahu on any given day, and their first experience of the islands is likely to be the capital city of Honolulu.

Downtown Honolulu is the site of the historic symbol of ancient Polynesian culture, Iolani Palace, where the last Hawaiian monarchs ruled before their kingdom was overthrown. Nearby stands a statue of King Kamehameha I. On June 11, Kamehameha Day, the statue is decorated with long flower leis. Behind the palace and dwarfing it is the state capitol, which was built in 1969.

Another interesting Honolulu site is Washington Place, a former home of Queen Liliuokalani that is now the residence of Hawaii's governor. Kawaiahao Church was designed by the Christian missionary Hiram Bingham in 1837 and was constructed from

Every June 11, long, glorious leis decorate Honolulu's statue of King Kamehameha I.

PLACES TO SEE

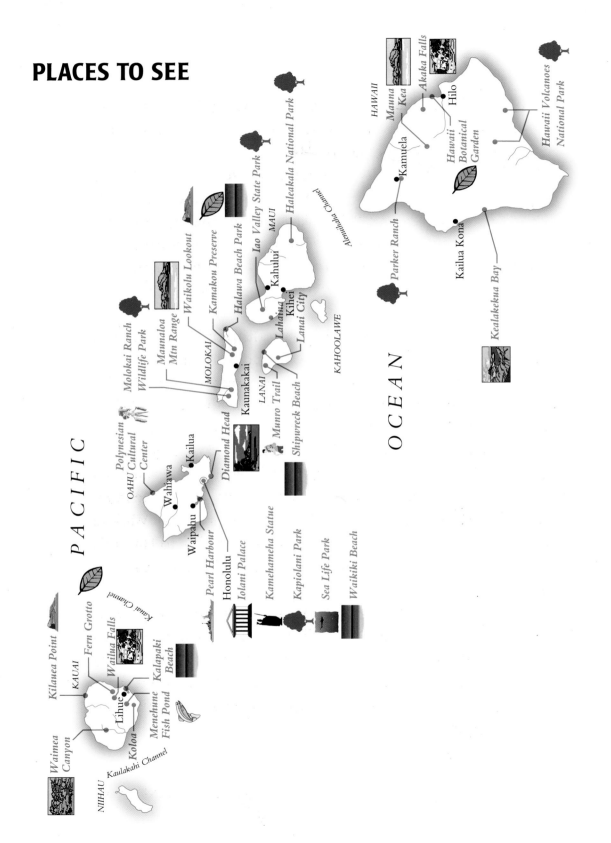

PACIFIC

OCEAN

KAUAI

Waimea Canyon

Kilauea Point

Fern Grotto

Wailua Falls

Kalapaki Beach

Lihue

Koloa

Menehune Fish Pond

Kaulakahi Channel

NIIHAU

Kauai Channel

OAHU

Polynesian Cultural Center

Wahiawa

Kailua

Waipahu

Pearl Harbour

Honolulu

Iolani Palace

Kamehameha Statue

Kapiolani Park

Sea Life Park

Waikiki Beach

Diamond Head

MOLOKAI

Molokai Ranch Wildlife Park

Maunaloa Mtn Range

Waikolu Lookout

Kamakou Preserve

Halawa Beach Park

Kaunakakai

LANAI

Munro Trail

Shipwreck Beach

Lanai City

MAUI

Iao Valley State Park

Haleakala National Park

Kahului

Lahaina

Kihei

KAHOOLAWE

Alenuihaha Channel

HAWAII

Mauna Kea

Akaka Falls

Hilo

Kamuela

Hawaii Botanical Garden

Hawaii Volcanoes National Park

Parker Ranch

Kailua Kona

Kealakekua Bay

large blocks of coral cut from nearby reefs. Along the city's southern shore is the famous natural feature Diamond Head, a remnant of an extinct crater 761 feet above the ocean.

Honolulu also has many fascinating museums. The Bishop Museum in particular should not be missed. It features frequently changing exhibitions about Polynesian culture. The museum also has a science center with a planetarium and observatory. The Honolulu Academy of Arts has an excellent collection of Asian art, as well as a fine collection of works by western Impressionist painters.

Waikiki Beach is a two-and-a-half-mile strip of sandy beaches, reefs, and coconut groves that has become a world-famous resort area. It became an important destination for tourists in the 1920s. Since the 1950s a line of large hotels, known as the "Great Wall of Waikiki," has encircled the beach. There are more than thirty thousand hotel rooms in the Waikiki area. Near the beach is the International Market Place, an acre of land devoted to restaurants and cafes, small shops, and kiosks selling tourist items. The more than eight hundred restaurants, bars, and clubs near Waikiki make it a place for people who prefer urban nightlife to Hawaii's tropical scenery, though the orange sunsets along Waikiki beach are magnificent.

Kapiolani Park is probably Honolulu's most popular park. It features tennis courts and baseball diamonds, as well as fields for other sports. The Royal Hawaiian Band plays here on Sunday afternoons, and traditional hula exhibitions are presented three times a week. There is also a large zoo, an aviary, an aquarium, and a rose garden.

Honolulu offers many interesting neighborhoods to explore, particularly Chinatown, where there are Buddhist temples, Taoist shrines, herb and noodle shops, and busy open-air markets. Another fascinating site is the Punchbowl, a volcanic crater where human sacrifices were once conducted by the ancient Polynesians. North of the Punchbowl is Nuuanu Pali Lookout, a cliff that offers magnificent views of the valleys north of the city.

HAWAII

Hawaii is the island to visit if you're interested in volcanoes. Its famous black sand beaches are made of lava that was broken up by the sea. One of the island's two main volcanoes, Mauna Kea, has been extinct for thousands of years. On its slopes you can find many ancient Polynesian temples and the Mauna Kea adze quarry, where the first Hawaiians mined a very hard basalt to make axes and other tools. Today, skiers take advantage of its snow-covered slopes. At the summit of Mauna Kea, scientists from the United States, Canada, England, and Japan have constructed nine huge astronomical telescopes. The newest is the Keck Observatory, which features the most powerful optical telescope in the world.

The other major volcano on the island of Hawaii, Mauna Loa, is not dormant. It has erupted thirty-six times in the last two centuries. Its last major eruption was in 1984, when lava flows stopped just five miles short of Hilo, the island's largest city. The west coast of Hawaii features large expanses of solidified lava from Mauna Loa's eruptions in 1907, 1919, 1926, and 1950.

East of Mauna Loa is Hawaii Volcanoes National Park and the

Hawaii's famed black sand beaches are made of pulverized lava.

crater of Kilauea volcano. Although Kilauea is not nearly as big as Mauna Kea and Mauna Loa, it is the most active volcano in the world. Fountains of fiery red lava and venting steam still pour forth from its caldera. "Imagine the Mississippi converted into liquid fire," said a witness to the 1840 eruption. At the southern edge of Kilauea is Halemaumau, the volcano's main vent, five hundred feet deep and bubbling with flaming rock.

Mauna Kea volcano is the site of many ancient temples, called heiaus.

Kilauea's fiery lava flows have become a tourist attraction. Harry Kim, who decides how close visitors can get, loves "giving mankind a once-in-a-lifetime experience of seeing a live volcano in action."

TEN LARGEST CITIES

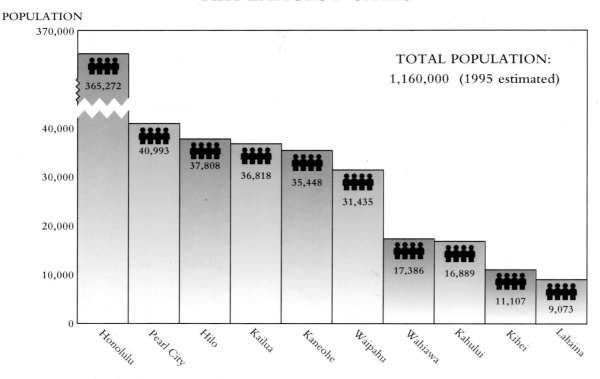

POPULATION

TOTAL POPULATION:
1,160,000 (1995 estimated)

City	Population
Honolulu	365,272
Pearl City	40,993
Hilo	37,808
Kailua	36,818
Kaneohe	35,448
Waipahu	31,435
Wahiawa	17,386
Kahului	16,889
Kihei	11,107
Lahaina	9,073

The city of Hilo, on the northeast coast, is the state's second-largest city, but it has not been built up with tourist hotels to the same extent as Honolulu. With its narrow streets and wooden houses, it has the appearance of a small, old-fashioned town. Tsunamis, or tidal waves, destroyed many of Hilo's buildings in 1946 and 1960, but much of the old historic district has been restored. Hilo is the center of the Hawaiian orchid industry. More than two thousand varieties of the flower adorn the city's many gardens and parks. Especially worth visiting are the Liliuokalani

Gardens. If you can get up early enough, it is also exciting to watch the morning auction at the Suisan Fish Market.

Driving north out of Hilo along the Hamakua coast toward the magnificent Waipio Valley, you can still see many old sugar plantations and the towns that were built to serve the cane workers. Macadamia nuts now grow on many of these plantations.

MAUI, MOLOKAI, AND KAUAI

Maui is the site of more astonishing volcanoes. Puu Kukui is almost six thousand feet tall, and Haleakala towers to just over ten thousand feet. The central crater of Haleakala is nearly three thousand feet deep and has a circumference of twenty-one miles. It is part of Haleakala National Park, which has many trails that can be traveled on foot or horseback. To see the sun rise from the summit of Haleakala is an awe-inspiring sight. At Haleakala's summit is Science City, a group of laboratories where scientists track military satellites and the University of Hawaii operates solar and lunar observatories.

Lahaina, on Maui's western coast, has been popular with visitors since the early nineteenth century, when it was a favorite port of call for the American whaling fleet. The town retains some of the atmosphere of that time, with a mixture of old houses and modern cafes, restaurants, boutiques, and art galleries. Whales are still often seen to the south of Lahaina, in Maalaea Bay.

Molokai is a small island west of Maui that is less than forty miles long and ten miles wide. It is a land of pineapple fields, taro patches, and cattle ranches. There are relatively few paved roads,

The world's largest dormant volcano, Haleakala crater, is twenty miles around.

and the population is less than seven thousand. The people of Molokai are committed to avoiding the kind of overdevelopment some of the other islands have suffered. Instead of building resorts, they want to develop hiking trails and camping areas. "By keeping Molokai unique, we will have a really good shot at attracting people in the future," says DeGray Vanderbilt, of the Molokai Chamber of Commerce. "But if we were to homogenize like the rest of the

WHALE WATCHING

Whale watching is a popular pastime for Hawaiians and visitors alike. The best areas are the shallow channels between the islands of Maui, Lanai, Molokai, and Kahoolawe and along the Kona coast of Hawaii. Some species, such as sperm whales and pilot whales, are seen around the islands throughout the year. But for many people, whale-watching season begins in November, when the humpback whales, which are more than forty feet long and weigh as much as sixty tons, migrate from the Arctic to their breeding grounds in the South Pacific. The humpbacks are known for their acrobatic leaps out of the water, which are part of their mating ritual. There are only about two thousand humpbacks left in the world, and they are protected by legislation. Because they are sensitive to human activity, it is illegal for boats to approach within one hundred yards of the magnificent beasts.

islands and roll over to indiscriminate development, we would be the big loser."

The most notable landmark of Molokai is the site of the former leper colony where Joseph de Veuster, who was known as Father Damien, the "Martyr of Molokai," went to work with the lepers in 1873. He himself died of leprosy in 1889. When the writer Robert Louis Stevenson visited the colony in 1889, he found it almost unbearably sorrowful. "They were strangers to each other," he

wrote about the lepers, "collected by common calamity, disfigured, mortally sick, banished without sin from home and friends."

Farther east, near the town of Halawa, some of the highest sea cliffs in the world tower above the waves, with several waterfalls that cascade more than a thousand feet down from the mountains.

The island of Kauai is a hiker's and naturalist's paradise. The high peaks at its center, Waialeale and Kawaikini, are bathed in nearly five hundred inches of rainfall a year, making this the wettest

The island of Molokai is noted for its stunning, unspoiled sea cliffs.

Kauai's lush mountains receive nearly ten feet of rain per year.

spot on the planet. The rains cascade down the western slopes of these peaks into the Alakai Swamp, a magnificent area of tropical rain forests and bogs where many of Hawaii's rarest trees and birds reside. Below the Alakai Swamp is Kokee State Park, which has wonderful views of the surrounding lowlands. The flow of water culminates in the Waimea Valley, a region of swamps and deep, lush valleys. In Lihue, the main town on the island, the Kauai Museum holds demonstrations of weaving and lei making.

LAST IMPRESSIONS

To visit Hawaii, then, is to confirm the images that millions of Americans hold of these beautiful islands. The state brings forth thoughts of a slightly mysterious paradise, a land of rugged volcanic mountains, dense tropical rain forests, coconut groves, flower leis, ancient legends of Polynesian kingdoms, and sunny beaches with pounding surf.

But Hawaii is more than the beautiful landscape and warm aloha spirit it shows to visitors. The mixture of Polynesian, Asian, and Caucasian faces in the streets tells us that Hawaii is a true melting pot. Halfway between the U.S. mainland and Asia, the state of Hawaii—in geography, in history, in culture—stands apart.

THE FLAG: The state flag of Hawaii contains both the British flag and the American flag. In the upper left-hand corner of the Hawaiian flag is the British Union Jack. The eight stripes of red, white and blue represent both the U.S. flag and the eight major Hawaiian islands. Designed about 1816 for King Kamehameha I of Hawaii, the flag was adopted in 1959 when Hawaii became the fiftieth state.

THE SEAL: In the middle of the seal is the state coat of arms, with King Kamehameha I on one side and the goddess of Liberty on the other. Around the two figures are taro and banana leaves, ferns, and a phoenix. The date 1959 is the year that Hawaii became a state and the seal was adopted. At the bottom, the state motto is written in Hawaiian.

STATE SURVEY

Statehood: August 21, 1959

Origin of Name: According to legend, Hawaii was named after a Polynesian chief, Hawaii-loa, who led the Polynesian settlers to the Hawaiian Islands. But legend also says that the name *Hawaii* may have come from *Hawaiki*, the name of the Polynesian homeland to the west.

Nickname: Aloha State

Capital: Honolulu (on the island of Oahu)

Motto: The life of the land is perpetuated in righteousness

Bird: Nene, or Hawaiian goose

Marine Mammal: Humpback whale

Flower: Yellow hibiscus

Tree: Kukui (candlenut tree)

Insect: Hawaiian fly

Nene

Yellow hibiscus

HAWAII PONOI

In 1874 "Hawaii Ponoi," composed by King David Kalakaua, was proclaimed the national anthem of the Kingdom of Hawaii. This song continued to be sung after the United States annexed the islands, and in 1967 the state legislature passed an act making it the state song.

Words by H.M. King Kalakaua

Music by H. Berger

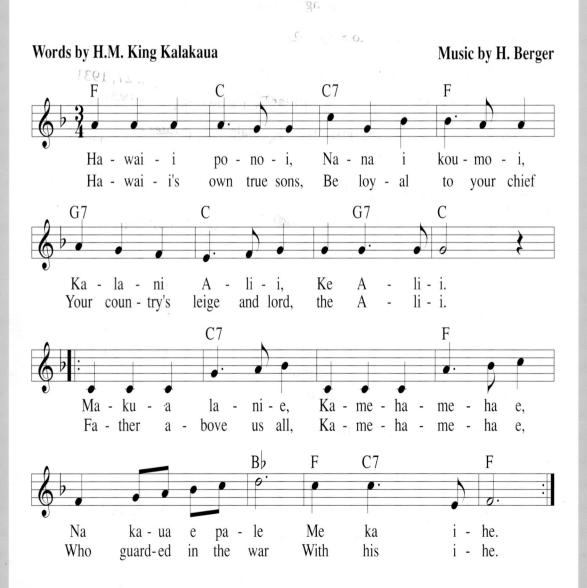

Ha - wai - i po - no - i, Na - na i kou - mo - i,
Ha - wai - i's own true sons, Be loy - al to your chief

Ka - la - ni A - li - i, Ke A - li - i.
Your coun - try's leige and lord, the A - li - i.

Ma - ku - a la - ni - e, Ka - me - ha - me - ha e,
Fa - ther a - bove us all, Ka - me - ha - me - ha e,

Na ka - ua e pa - le Me ka i - he.
Who guard - ed in the war With his i - he.

GEOGRAPHY

Highest Point: 13,796 feet above sea level, at Mauna Kea

Lowest Point: Sea level along coast

Area: 6,459 square miles, including 36 square miles of inland water

Greatest Distance, North to South: 230 miles

Greatest Distance, East to West: 350 miles

Hottest Recorded Temperature: 100°F at Pahala on April 27, 1931

Coldest Recorded Temperature: 14°F at Haleakala Crater on January 2, 1961

Average Annual Precipitation: 110 inches

Major Islands: Hawaii (the Big Island), Kahoolawe, Kauai, Lanai, Maui, Molokai, Niihau, and Oahu

Ocean: Pacific

Most Active Volcano: Kilauea (on Hawaii)

Trees: ash, bamboo, banana, banyon, cedar, coconut, cypress, guava, juniper, kiawe, koa, kukui (candlenut), mango, noni, Norfolk pine, ohia, palm, papaya, redwood, sandalwood, sugi

Plants: fern, kaunaoa, olona, panini, pineapple, prickly pear cactus, sugarcane (grass), taro, ti

Flowers: African violet, anthurium, carnation, frangipani, hibiscus, hydrangea, ilima, lantana, lobelia, lokelani, morning glory, orchid, passion flower, protea, silversword

Fruits: banana, breadfruit, coconut, guava, kiwi, kumquat, lime, litchi, mango, orange, papaya, passion fruit, pineapple, plum

Animals: axis deer, cattle, chicken, coral, crab, dog, donkey, goat, Hawaiian fly, hawksbill turtle, hoary bat, horse, lobster, mongoose, sheep, shrimp (prawns), snail, wild boar

Marine Mammals: dolphin, monk seal, whale

Birds: akepa, albatross, amakihi, 'a'o, cardinal, coot, crow, duck, elepaio, finch, frigate, Hawaiian honeycreeper, hawk, heron, 'i'iwi, millerbird, moorhen, myna, nene (Hawaiian goose), noddy, owl, palila, parrotbill, peacock, petrel, plover, poouli, red-footed booby, shearwater, stilt, tern, thrush, white-tailed tropic bird

Fish: ahi, a'u, barracuda, gray snapper, mahimahi (dolphin fish), marlin, ono, rectangular triggerfish, sailfish, shark, swordfish, tuna, ulua

Endangered Animals: achatinellid land snail, amastrid land snail, coot, crow, Hawaiian honeycreeper, hawk, hawksbill turtle, helcinid land snail, humpback whale, Laysan duck, Laysan fish, Maui akepa, monk seal, moorhen, Nihoa fish, Nihoa millerbird, Oahu tree snail, palila, parrotbill, poouli, stilt

Hawksbill turtle

Endangered Plants and Areas: eke silversword, mixed sedge and grass montane bog, 'ohi'a lowland mesic forest, olupua/lama lowland dry forest

TIMELINE

Hawaii History

c. 5 B.C. Polynesians from Pacific Islands come to Hawaii

c. 1200 Polynesians from Tahiti settle on Hawaii and take over the islands

1778 Captain Cook reaches Hawaii

1795 King Kamehameha I unites the Hawaiian Islands

1820 Protestant missionaries arrive on the island

1835 Hawaii starts the first sugar plantation, on Kauai Island

1840 First written constitution grants powers to elected legislature

1854 People from other countries begin coming to Hawaii to work on the plantations

1874 King Kalakaua restores Hawaiian customs

1875 Reciprocity treaty signed with the United States

c. 1885 The Hawaiian pineapple industry is founded

1887 Hawaiian League imposes "Bayonet Constitution" on King Kalakaua, which gives the U.S. Navy exclusive use of Pearl Harbor as a port

1893 A group of Americans and Europeans overthrows Queen Liliuokalani

1894 Hawaii becomes a republic; an American, Sanford B. Dole, becomes Hawaii's first and only president

1898 The United States annexes Hawaii

1900 Hawaii becomes a U.S. territory; Hawaiians become U.S. citizens

1908 U.S. Congress authorizes building of naval base at Pearl Harbor

1919 Jonah Kuhio Kalanianaole, Hawaii's delegate to Congress, introduces first statehood bill

1934 President Franklin D. Roosevelt is the first U.S. president to visit Hawaii

1941 The Japanese attack Pearl Harbor; the United States enters World War II

1959 Hawaii becomes the fiftieth state

1992 Hurricane Iniki hits Hawaii, causing four deaths and $2 billion in damage

1993 President Bill Clinton signs U.S. Public Law 103-150, which acknowledges that the overthrow of Queen Liliuokalani and the Hawaiian monarchy in 1893 by American businessmen and U.S. Marines was illegal

1994 Groups seeking Hawaiian independence issue the Proclamation of Restoration of Independence of the Sovereign Nation State of Hawaii

1995 Groups agree on a new constitution for the nation of Hawaii, though the document does not have legal force

ECONOMY

Agricultural Products: avocados, bananas, beef, cattle, chicken, coffee, corn, dairy products, eggs, fish, flowers, guavas, hogs, honey, kiwis, macadamia nuts, papayas, passion fruit, pineapples, potatoes, prawns, sugarcane

Harvesting pineapple

Manufactured Products: chemicals, clothing, cocoa beans (chocolate), concrete, food processing (including refined sugar, canned pineapple, and fruit juices), perfume, petroleum processing, printed materials

Natural Resources: coral, crushed stone, pearls, sand, shells, titanium oxide (a paint pigment)

Business and Trade: communications, including newspapers in many languages and radio and television stations; finance, insurance, and real estate; service industries, including the armed forces, hospitals, hotels, law firms, and rental car agencies; tourism; transportation, including airlines, shipping, and trucking

CALENDAR OF CELEBRATIONS

Chinese New Year This festival comes in mid-January or February; visitors line the streets of Honolulu's Chinatown to watch the colorful lion dances in the Chinese New Year parade.

Narcissus Festival As part of the Chinese New Year celebrations, this festival on Oahu runs for about five weeks and includes arts and crafts, food booths, and even a ball.

Ka Molokai Makahiki Every January, the island of Molokai holds a modern-day version of the old makahiki festival. The week-long celebration begins with a fishing contest using canoes and ends with a tournament of Hawaiian games and sports. Hula dancers perform on the last day.

Cherry Blossom Festival From late January until March, Honolulu hosts this Japanese festival that includes tea ceremonies, beautiful flowers, and special drummers.

Captain Cook Festival Captain Cook is celebrated on Kauai every February with food, entertainment, and a foot race.

Oahu Kite Festival This weekend event of colorful kite-flying is held in early March at Kapiolani Park in Waikiki. Both professional and amateur kite-fliers take part in the fun.

Prince Kuhio Day Every March 26, residents celebrate the birthday of Prince Kuhio, a Hawaiian royal prince and Hawaii's first member of the U.S. Congress. Celebrations are held on Oahu and also on Kauai, the prince's birthplace.

"Merrie Monarch" Festival Beginning on Easter Sunday, Hilo, on the Big Island, hosts this week-long festival celebrating King David Kalakaua, the "Merrie Monarch," who brought back the hula to his people. Hawaii's largest hula contest is the main attraction.

May Day May Day is Lei Day in Hawaii; everyone celebrates this holiday on May 1 by wearing a lei. Lei-making contests are held on most of the islands.

Molokai Ka Hula Piko This festival on Molokai in mid-May celebrates the hula with dance performances and Hawaiian food.

King Kamehameha Day All of Hawaii celebrates the birthday of King Kamehameha I on June 11, a state holiday. Part of the fun includes covering the statues of King Kamehameha with 12-foot leis.

King Kamehameha Day

International Festival of the Pacific This festival in mid-July in Hilo, on the Big Island, has a "Pageant of Nations," with folk dances and costumes from Asia and the Pacific.

Prince Lot Hula Festival On Oahu on the third Saturday in July, students from Hawaii's most popular hula schools enter hula contests.

Annual Ukulele Festival Ukulele music is celebrated in late July; hundreds of ukulele players come to Waikiki's Kapiolani Park Bandstand for this yearly event.

Obon Season This Japanese festival honoring ancestors is celebrated around the islands in July and August. The final event of the celebration is the famous floating lantern ceremony along Waikiki's Ala Wai Canal on the night of August 15.

Admission Day Held on the third Friday in August, this state holiday celebrates the day Hawaii became a state. Hula and lei-making workshops are held on the Big Island.

Aloha Week For a week in September or October, the islands come alive with celebrations of Hawaiian culture, including Hawaiian sports, games, crafts, food, music, and dance.

Annual Kona Coffee Festival Coffee is celebrated for two weeks in Kailua-Kona, on the Big Island, the only place where coffee is grown in the United States. A parade in late October or early November and a coffee-picking contest are part of the entertainment.

STATE STARS

Heinrich (Henry) Berger (1844–1929) of Germany came to Hawaii in 1868 to lead the Royal Hawaiian Band. Berger led the band for 30 years and became known as the father of Hawaiian music for the more than 1,000 Hawaiian songs he arranged for band performance. With King David Kalakaua, he wrote "Hawaii Ponoi," the national anthem, which later became Hawaii's state song.

Heinrich Berger

Hiram Bingham (1789–1869) became known for leading a group of Protestant missionaries to Hawaii in 1820. With some of these missionaries, Bingham created an alphabet for the Hawaiian language and helped

Hiram Bingham

translate the Bible into Hawaiian. Bingham was the grandfather of Hiram Bingham (1875-1956), who was born in Honolulu and went on to discover the Inca city of Machu Picchu, in the Andes Mountains of Peru.

Charles Reed Bishop (1822–1915) was born in New York but became a banker in Hawaii. Bishop gave a great deal of money to Hawaii to improve its schools.

Benjamin Cayetano (1939–   ) is the first Filipino American to hold office in the United States. As governor of Hawaii, Cayetano is known for his support of Hawaii's tourist industry.

James Cook (1728–1779), an English explorer, was the first European to set foot on Hawaii. Cook was a captain in the British navy when, in 1778, he landed in the Hawaiian Islands. He called them the Sandwich Islands, after the Earl of Sandwich. A year later, Cook was killed by a group of Hawaiians who were angry at his treatment of them.

Joseph de Veuster (1840–1889) was a Belgian missionary who cared for lepers in the leper colony on Molokai. De Veuster was known as Father Damien, or the "Martyr of Molokai," for his great work. He himself died of leprosy, or Hansen's disease, as it is now called.

James Dole (1877–1958) was the son of Sanford Dole, president of the Republic of Hawaii. In 1922, James Dole set up a 15,000-acre pineapple plantation on Lanai, which is sometimes called Pineapple Island. Dole is famous for having established the pineapple industry in Hawaii.

Sanford Dole (1844–1926) was the first and only president of the Republic of Hawaii. In 1893, Dole led a small group who removed Queen Liliuokalani from the throne. A year later, he became Hawaii's president. Dole also served as the first governor of the territory of Hawaii.

Arthur Godfrey (1903–1983) was a television star in the 1950s and 1960s who made Hawaiian music and Hawaiian culture popular throughout the United States. The Hawaiian entertainer Don Ho was a frequent guest on Godfrey's TV show and Arthur Godfrey's colorful Hawaiian shirts and ukulele playing gave audiences a taste of Hawaii.

Don Ho (1930–   ) has done more than anyone else to keep Hawaiian music alive. Ho is the best-known Hawaiian entertainer. His shows for tourists in Hawaii, especially in Honolulu, and his many appearances on television programs have made him popular throughout the United States.

Daniel Inouye (1924–   ), born in Honolulu, is the first Japanese American to serve in the U.S. Congress. During his long career, Inouye has served in the Hawaiian house of representatives and the Hawaiian senate. In 1959, he became Hawaii's first U.S. representative to Congress. Later, he was elected to the U.S. Senate. Inouye gained national fame by serving on the committee that investigated the Watergate scandal of President Richard M. Nixon's administration.

Duke Kahanamoku (1890-1968), the famous Hawaiian surfer, was known as the human fish for his achievements in surfing, swimming, and water polo. A medal-winning swimmer in the 1912, 1920, and 1924 Olympics,

Duke also played on the Olympic water polo team in 1932 at the age of forty-two. Although a great swimmer, Duke is best known for his surfing tricks, such as riding backward and doing handstands on his board, maneuvers that earned him the title "the father of modern surfing." He also served as sheriff of Honolulu for twenty-nine years.

David Kalakaua (1836–1891), known as the "Merrie Monarch," was king of Hawaii from 1874 to 1891. With his wife, Queen Kapiolani, Kalakaua encouraged his people to keep Hawaiian customs alive. King Kalakaua's "merry" deeds included bringing back Hawaiian music and the hula. With Heinrich Berger he wrote "Hawaii Ponoi," the national anthem, which later became the state song.

David Kalakaua

Kamehameha I (1758?–1819), also known as Kamehameha the Great, was the founder of the kingdom of Hawaii. Kamehameha I was king when Captain Cook landed in Hawaii in 1778. By 1810, he had united all the Hawaiian Islands. The son of a chief, he took the name Kamehameha, meaning "the one set apart."

Kamehameha II (1797–1824) ruled Hawaii from 1819 to 1824. Although he was a son of Kamehameha I (the Great), he was not a strong ruler. During his reign, the ancient kapu system of taboos was eliminated, leading the way for American missionaries to come to Hawaii. He died of measles while visiting King George of England.

Kamehameha II

Kamehameha III (1813–1854) was a son of Kamehameha I (the Great) and a younger brother of Kamehameha II. At the age of 12, upon the death of Kamehameha II, he took over the throne of Hawaii, ruling until 1854. In 1840, he set up the first Hawaiian constitution, which later gave Hawaiians the right to vote, to own land, and to share power with the king.

Kamehameha IV (1834–1863), also known as Alexander Liholiho, was king of Hawaii from 1854 to 1863. He was the grandson of Kamehameha I (the Great) and the nephew and adopted son of Kamehameha III. During his reign, Hawaiians were dying from illnesses brought to the islands from Europe. As a result, Kamehameha IV built the Queen's Hospital in Honolulu to care for sick people. When his only child died in 1862, he left the throne.

Kamehameha V

Kamehameha V (1830–1872), also known as Lot Kamehameha, was the last of the Kamehameha kings. An older brother of Kamehameha IV, he ruled Hawaii from 1863 to 1872. During his reign, a new constitution was approved by Hawaiians and sugarcane became an important crop. The king died on his birthday, December 11. He had never married and had no heir to the throne. David Kalakaua became king upon his death.

Lydia Liliuokalani (1838–1917) was the last of the Hawaiian kings and queens. After her brother, King David Kalakaua, died, Liliuokalani tried to bring back power to the Hawaiian throne. But American settlers who owned most of Hawaii's resources overthrew her, and Hawaii became a republic. The queen, who ruled only two years, from 1891 to 1893, is remembered for her song, "Aloha Oe," which became Hawaii's song of farewell.

Bette Midler (1945–   ), born in Honolulu, Hawaii, is one of the best-known female entertainers in the United States. Midler's forceful singing style and talented acting in such films as *The Rose* have made her an international celebrity.

Ellison Shoji Onizuka (1946-1986), the first Hawaiian astronaut, was one of the seven people to die in the explosion aboard the space shuttle *Challenger* in 1986. A hero to people across the nation, Onizuka became the first Japanese American to make a flight into space. During his trip aboard the space shuttle *Discovery* in 1985, Onizuka realized the risks of space flight. After the trip he told reporters, "You're really aware that you're on top of a monster; you're totally at the mercy of the vehicle."

John McAllister Schofield (1831–1906) was a Union general during the Civil War. In 1872, he visited Pearl Harbor and realized its importance as a U.S. military base. Later, Schofield Barracks in Hawaii was named after him. During the Japanese attack on Pearl Harbor on December 7, 1941, Schofield Barracks was hit, but not destroyed, by Japanese aircraft.

Cathy Song (1955–   ), a native of Honolulu, is one of the most popular young poets in the United States. Song's two books of poetry, *Picture Bride* (1983) and *Frameless Windows, Squares of Light* (1988), are filled with beautiful visual images and with memories of her childhood. As a creative-writing teacher and a poet, Song stresses the importance of writing about cultural heritage and personal experiences.

John L. Stevens (1820–1895) was a U.S. envoy (diplomat) to Hawaii from 1889 to 1893. Stevens played a large part in the 1893 rebellion to remove

John L. Stevens

Queen Liliuokalani from the throne. He was also involved in setting up the new government under Sanford B. Dole.

Kathleen Tyau (1946–   ) has done much in her writing to depict the Hawaiian way of life. A native of Oahu, Tyau's funny novel *A Little Too Much Is Enough* describes Hawaiian delights, from making poi to eating a nine-course wedding feast.

John Waihee (1946–   ), born in Honokaa, is the first Hawaiian governor of Polynesian descent. During his term, from 1986 to 1994, Hawaii became the first state to adopt universal health care. Waihee also took a strong stand on protecting Hawaii's fragile environment.

TOUR THE STATE

OAHU

Waikiki Beach (Honolulu) This busy beach has high-rise hotels, beautiful orange sunsets, swimmers, surfers, and plenty of tourists.

Kapiolani Park (Honolulu) King Kalakaua gave this 200-acre park to the people of Honolulu in 1877. The park has an aquarium, a zoo, hula show grounds, a bandstand, tennis courts, and space for kite flying.

Iolani Palace (Honolulu) Once the home of Hawaiian kings and queens, this is the only royal palace in the United States. Today, the palace offers guided tours through its throne room, palace grounds, and museum.

Kamehameha Statue (Honolulu) The statue of Kamehameha I (the Great) stands opposite Iolani Palace and is a popular tourist spot. It is especially popular on June 11, the king's birthday, when people dress the statue in leis.

Pearl Harbor (Pearl Harbor area) Visitors can still see the sunken battleship *Arizona*, which was attacked by the Japanese on December 7, 1941.

Diamond Head (Southeast Oahu) This 760-foot-high volcano was named by British sailors who thought that the sparkling crystals on top of the volcano were diamonds. A hiking trail to the top of Diamond Head offers a great view of the island.

Sea Life Park (Southeast Oahu) Fish, sea turtles, eels, hammerhead sharks, Hawaiian monk seals, and performing dolphins and whales can be seen at Hawaii's only marine park.

Polynesian Cultural Center (Windward Coast) This reconstruction of villages from Samoa, New Zealand, Fiji, Tahiti, Tonga, the Marquesas, and Hawaii has huts, weavings, tapa cloth, crafts, and Polynesian dances and games.

Dole Pineapple Pavilion (Central Oahu) Pineapple fields, a pineapple processing plant, and a free cup of pineapple juice make this a popular place to visit.

HAWAII—THE BIG ISLAND

Kealakekua Bay (South Kona) A monument marks the place where Captain James Cook was killed on February 14, 1779.

Puako Petroglyphs (north of Kona) Here you can see one of the largest

Petroglyphs

and oldest collections of petroglyphs (lava carvings of humans, animals, objects, and shapes) found in Hawaii.

Parker Ranch Visitor Center and Museum (Waimea) Visitors to this huge ranch can tour two historic homes and a museum. They are filled with paintings, photographs, quilts, old saddles, and surfboards.

Hawaii Tropical Botanical Garden (Hamakua Coast) Thousands of tropical plants, lush streams and waterfalls, and a lily pond make this garden in a rain forest a beautiful place to visit.

Mauna Kea (Mauna Kea) Adventurous visitors can reach the summit of Hawaii's highest mountain by taking a six-mile hike. An incredible glacier can be seen on the way to the top.

Hawaii Volcanoes National Park (near Pahala) This unique national park has two active volcanoes, a steaming crater (Kilauea Caldera), lava flows, a desert, and beautiful beaches.

MAUI

Lahaina (western Maui) Once the royal court of Maui chiefs and a whaling town, Lahaina has some of the best sightseeing spots in Hawaii, including the Pioneer Inn, the whaling museum, and the old mission.

Iao Valley State Park (Wailuku area) Iao Needle rises more than a thousand feet into the air and is a treat for amateur photographers visiting this state park.

Haleakala National Park (Haleakala) Haleakala Crater is the main view in this amazing national park, named for Haleakala, the world's largest inactive volcano. Spectacular sunrises at the rim of the crater earn Haleakala its name, "House of the Sun."

MOLOKAI

Palaau State Park (Central Molokai) A five-minute walk from the parking lot, Kalaupapa Overlook is the main attraction in this state park. This 1,600-foot cliff offers an aerial view of Kalaupapa Peninsula without the airplane!

Waikolu Lookout (Central Molokai) At 3,600 feet, this lookout point gives visitors an awesome view of Waikolu Valley and the ocean beyond.

Kamakou Preserve (Central Molokai) Just beyond Waikolu Lookout is Kamakou Preserve, a rain forest with many rare and endangered plants and animals.

Maunaloa (West End) This mountain range lives up to its name, which means "Long Mountain." Its highest point is Puunana, at 1,381 feet.

Molokai Ranch Wildlife Park (West End) Zebras, giraffes, wild turkeys, elands, and other animals from Africa, India, Asia, and South America have been brought to the park to roam its 350 acres. It is a popular place for tourists and U.S. and Japanese film crews.

LANAI

Lanai City (Central Lanai) A new tourist attraction, this once-bustling plantation town still has some pineapple fields, tin-roofed houses, brightly painted buildings, lush yellow flowers, and Dole Park, which is lined with tall Norfolk pines.

Munro Trail (Northwest Lanai) You can walk this 8½-mile dirt road in a day and can see most of the Hawaiian Islands from various points along the route.

KAUAI

Menehune Fish Pond (East Side) The misty Haupu Ridge in the background and the stone wall that is said to have been built by the menehunes (the "little people" of Hawaiian myth) make this fish pond a mysterious place to visit.

Wailua Falls (East Side) This scenic 80-foot waterfall lies at the edge of a sugarcane field.

Fern Grotto (East Side) The riverboat tour up the Wailua River to the Fern Grotto, a cave beneath a fern-covered rock face, is Kauai's busiest and most romantic tourist attraction.

Kilauea Point (North Shore) This wildlife refuge, topped by an old lighthouse, has the look of a picture postcard.

Koloa (South Shore) Hawaii's first sugar plantation was started in Koloa in 1835. Sugarcane fields, sugar exhibits, and the old town make interesting sights.

Waimea Canyon (West Side) This canyon, which is nicknamed the Grand Canyon of the Pacific, earns its name with a colorful river-cut gorge, beautiful waterfalls, and deep-red earth.

FIND OUT MORE

FIND OUT MORE

If you would like to learn more about Hawaii, look in your library, bookstore, or video store for these titles:

STATE BOOKS

Fradin, Dennis. *Hawaii*. Chicago: Children's Press, 1994.

Johnston, Joyce. *Hawaii*. Minneapolis: Lerner, 1995.

McNair, Sylvia. *America the Beautiful: Hawaii*. Chicago: Children's Press, 1990.

SPECIAL INTEREST BOOKS

Ackerman, Diane. *Monk Seal Hideaway*. New York: Crown, 1995.

Feeney, Stephanie, and Ann Fielding. *Sand to Sea: Marine Life of Hawaii*. Honolulu: University of Hawaii Press, 1989.

Haney, David. *Captain Cook and the Explorers of the Pacific*. New York: Chelsea House, 1992.

Papastavrou, Vassili. *Whale*. New York: Alfred A. Knopf, 1993.

Takaki, Ronald. *Raising Cane: The World of Plantation Hawaii*. New York: Chelsea House, 1994.

Wardlaw, Lee. *Cowabunga! The Complete Book of Surfing*. New York: Avon, 1991.

FICTION

Okimoto, Jean Davies. *Who Did It, Jenny Lake?* New York: Putnam, 1983.

Salisbury, Graham. *Blue Skin of the Sea*. New York: Delacorte, 1992.

————. *Under the Blood-Red Sun*. New York: Delacorte, 1994.

VIDEOTAPES

Discover Hawaii. 120 minutes. Reader's Digest, 1990.

Hawaii. 60 minutes. International Video Corp., 1992.

Hawaii: The Pacific Paradise. 120 minutes. Questar Video, Inc., 1994.

WEBSITES

You also might want to check the Internet for these sites, which are run by the Hawaiian government:

www.state.hi.us

www.hawaii.gov

INDEX

Page numbers for illustrations are in boldface.